Jacobo Schifter, PhD

Lila's House
Male Prostitution in Latin America

Pre-publication
REVIEWS,
COMMENTARIES,
EVALUATIONS . . .

"**L***ila's House* is an important new addition to the rapidly growing literature about same-sex relations and emerging gay communities in Latin America. In this detailed empirical study of the lives of young male sex workers in San José, Costa Rica, Jacobo Schifter documents the constitution of a changing sexual subculture in which the dilemmas of desire, poverty, stigma, and resistance constantly intersect in the flow of daily life. Unflinching in his willingness to confront realities that might unsettle or repulse less courageous researchers, Schifter entreats his readers to approach this book with an open heart. These are surely the key qualities with which he has approached the young men who are the subjects of this study, men whose lives and experiences have been marked by so many forms of oppression and injustice. This is a poignant and courageous book!"

Richard G. Parker, PhD
Associate Professor of Public Health,
Columbia University,
New York

More pre-publication
REVIEWS, COMMENTARIES, EVALUATIONS . . .

" **I** n this highly readable text, Dr. Schifter explores and explodes the myths surrounding male prostitution. Using case studies and live interviews, Schifter gives us insights into the *cachero* (male prostitute) mentality in Central America that no outsider to the region could have uncovered. This study exposes the dangerous and often contradictory lives of young males who sell their bodies for a better life."

Wayne M. Bryant
Bisexual Resource Center,
Board of Directors;
Author of *Bisexual Characters in Film: From Anaïs to Zee*

" **I** found Jacobo Schifter's study of male brothel prostitution in Costa Rica to be innovative and pathbreaking. Male prostitution is a subject much talked about, but on which there has been little research. The fact that the study took place in a brothel makes it even more pathbreaking, since what studies we do have are primarily of street prostitution. The prostitutes, ranging in age from thirteen to twenty-seven, did not, for the most part, consider themselves homosexuals. Rather they were *cacheros,* men who have sex with other men for pleasure or money, but when they do so they are the penetrators. This attitude conforms with the general cultural assumptions of most of Spanish-speaking Latin America, that only equates homosexuality with effeminate behavior and being penetrated. The author claims that many of the clients were pedophiles and the evidence he gives on these little-understood men should prove useful in trying to explain the phenomenon. The great value of the study is in giving us a cross-cultural look at male prostitution, allowing us to compare it to what we know about male prostitution in the United States and elsewhere. It emphasizes that explanations for prostitution, while based on economic factors, are many and varied. In short it is a fascinating, informative study that should become a classic."

Vern L. Bullough, PhD, RN
Visiting Professor,
University of Southern California

" **A** quite extraordinary book that provides graphic insight into aspects of sexual life so frequently stereotyped and misunderstood."

Professor Peter Aggleton
Tomas Coram Research Unit,
University of London

Harrington Park Press
An Imprint of The Haworth Press, Inc.

Lila's House
Male Prostitution in Latin America

HAWORTH Gay & Lesbian Studies
John P. De Cecco, PhD
Editor in Chief

Lila's House
Male Prostitution in Latin America

Jacobo Schifter, PhD

Translated by
Irene Artavia Fernández
Sharon Mulheren

Harrington Park Press
An Imprint of The Haworth Press, Inc.
New York • London

Published by

Harrington Park Press, an imprint of The Haworth Press, Inc., 10 Alice Street, Binghamton, NY 13904-1580

Cover design by Marylouise E. Doyle.

The Library of Congress has cataloged the hardcover edition of this book as:

Schifter, Jacobo.
    [Casa de Lila. English]
    Lila's house : male prostitution in Latin America / Jacobo Schifter.
        p.   cm.
    Includes bibliographical references and index.
    ISBN 0-7890-0593-X (alk. paper).
    1. Male prostitution—Costa Rica—San José. 2. Male prostitutes—Costa Rica—San José.
I. Title.
HQ154.A5S3413   1998
306.74′2′0972863—dc21   98-26319
                                                                        CIP

ISBN 1-56023-943-3 (pbk.)

I feel the pain again
here, now, in this place.
I take the path of the mirror,
I stop at the threshold,
I look at it and I see the reflection;

Your reflection

I cannot identify
what I feel,
or what I see,
or what you are trying to tell me.

You speak a language that is difficult
to understand.

—Antonio Bustamante

ABOUT THE AUTHOR

Jacobo Schifter, PhD, is currently the Regional Director of ILPES (The Latin American Health and Prevention Institute), an AIDS prevention program financed by the Netherlands' government. His initial publications included *The Hidden Face of the Costa Rican Civil War* (1979), two books on U.S.-Costa Rican relations, and one on Costa Rican antisemitism. However, once AIDS began to impact Central America, Dr. Schifter shifted interests and established the first regional institute to fight the epidemic, as well as created dozens of innovative programs, such as AIDS hotlines, AIDS prevention workshops for Latin gays, prisoners, street children, Indians, male sex workers, and other minority groups. Dr. Schifter has published many other controversial, best-selling books, such as *The Formation of a Counterculture: AIDS and Homosexuality in Costa Rica* (1989), *Men Who Love Men* (1992), *Eyes That Do Not See: Psychiatry and Homophobia* (1997). In 1997, he was asked by the University of London to participate in an anthology on male prostitution and HIV infection, which led to this study of the unexplored world of male prostitution in a Latin context.

CONTENTS

Foreword

I first met Jacobo Schifter at a conference on AIDS hot lines organized by the Dutch Government and the European Commission in Curacao in 1990. He introduced himself, and presented me with an interesting project proposal in the area of AIDS prevention. I glanced at it, but did not give it much thought at the time; as the representative of a donor country, one receives many such proposals during the course of an international conference.

However, upon my return to the Netherlands, I started to read the document with growing interest. Not only had I come across some of Jacobo's other work on gay men and the Costa Rican Jewish community, but I was intrigued by his unconventional and highly original approach to AIDS prevention.

It was on the strength of this proposal that the Dutch Government first became involved in prevention work in the Central American region, and what began as a simple telephone hot line (Con Voz) soon blossomed into a highly enterprising, action-oriented organization known as the Latin American Institute for Health Prevention and Education (ILPES).

Moreover, at a personal level, I would like to stress the degree to which Jacobo's writings on sexuality and minority empowerment have influenced my own work in developing countries, both by providing me with a better understanding of human behavior, and by challenging me to find new ways of opening up bureaucratic systems to innovation and creativity.

In this book, we find the author at his best. Casting aside the trappings of false neutrality, Jacobo becomes actively engaged with his subject matter, while at the same time proving to be an articulate defender of the human rights of those whom *Lila's House* is about. However, this is not to suggest that the book is merely an account of the relentless discrimination faced by a community relegated to the margins of social life. At a broader level, it also offers readers an incisive exploration of the relationship between adolescent sexual development and a cultural context that remains heavily inscribed with the social mores of the nineteenth century. Moreover, by calling into question our assumptions and fixed ideas about sex and sexual orientation, Jacobo provides us with useful tools in the fight against HIV/AIDS, both in Costa Rica and in Latin America more generally.

Thus, given the undoubted significance of Jacobo's contributions, let us hope that more of his writings are translated into other languages; the world can only benefit by becoming familiar with them.

Hans Moerkerk
Ministry of Foreign Affairs,
The Netherlands

Acknowledgments

Many people have helped make this study possible. First of all, Peter Aggleton of the University of London convinced me to conduct a study on male prostitution for an anthology to be published in the United Kingdom by UCL Press. Peter Aggleton helped me translate a short version of the study into English, and participated as editor and co-author. His suggestions were extremely helpful in improving the manuscript.

Antonio Bustamante coordinated the data collection phase, made the initial contacts, obtained permission to enter Lila's house, and served as a consultant on the topic of *cacherismo* in Central America.

Lidia Montero helped transcribe the interviews, an extremely tedious job because of the enormous volume of material gathered.

My friend and collaborator at ILPES' Research Department, Johnny Madrigal, MSc, made excellent suggestions and gave the final approval before the book was sent to the publisher.

Without Lila and the young men, this project would never have been possible. Despite the risks for everyone involved, their collaboration has left me deeply indebted to them. ILPES' launch of a prevention program and the opening of a clubhouse for sex workers are small tokens of my appreciation.

Julián González, a linguistics specialist and one of the best editors in the country helped eliminate much of the "Spanglish" that I learned during my time in the United States.

Hector Elizondo, coordinator of ILPES Group 2828, who works with groups of gay sex workers was, as always, the first to give me the green light for publication. His sixth sense for literature and his ability to tell me what he does not like is, for me, irreplaceable.

Nevertheless, the responsibility for what is written in this book is mine and mine alone. My interpretations do not represent any official position of the Institute, the donor, any of my co-workers who collaborated on this project, or the publisher.

Many thanks to all of you. And to the readers, I ask you to read this book with an open mind and an open heart.

Introduction

Why Write About the Forbidden?

Male prostitution is as old as female prostitution. As far back as the Sumerians and the Greeks, evidence exists that men sold sexual services to other men.[1] However, little is known about male prostitution. In his book *Male Prostitution*, published in 1993, Donald J. West affirms that "popular wisdom about male prostitution is confused and contradictory, poorly informed, and generally more concerned with moral judgment than with humane understanding.[2] Female prostitution, on the other hand, has received more attention from researchers and the public in general; so much so, in fact, that as an institution, prostitution is associated with women.[3] In patriarchal societies where service work is associated with women, men who serve other men are seen as doing "women's work."[4] In Costa Rica, one of the characteristics associated with femininity is sexual servitude to men.[5] Male prostitution, however, was known among the Greeks, and was even taxed during Augustus's reign in Rome.[6] Despite its longevity, it still remains hidden.

Recent literature is full of stereotypes concerning male prostitution. Richie McMullen[7] describes prostitutes as young homosexual men looking for love and friendship, like other gay young men. However, the former have had the misfortune to choose prostitution as a temporary means of survival, in the face of difficult economic circumstances.

Another stereotype is that of a young man who runs away from his home and falls into the clutches of adult gay men who exploit him and take advantage of his innocence.[8] Yet another is that of the juvenile delinquent looking for easy money to complement other illicit activities, such as theft and swindling, thereby displaying poor judgment and a lack of maturity. There are innumerable examples of family rejection and self-destructive behavior.[9]

Very few studies on male prostitution have gone beyond sex workers on the street. For example, in a study of street prostitutes in the United States, Allen was surprised by the presence of many middle-class young men, who came to the profession more by choice than by necessity.[10] Studies carried out at the South Bank Polytechnic in the United Kingdom reveal the wide variety of male prostitution services available in England, which include men of different social groups.[11] Finally, West conducted an analysis of the wide range of sex workers who attend a medical support project known as the Streetwise Youth Day Centre in London. West challenges the myth that all prostitutes are delinquent homosexual youths from broken homes. On the contrary, he found young middle-class men, both heterosexual and bisexual, ranging from illiterates to wealthy men living in luxurious houses. Among the sex workers he interviewed, there was no "typical" prostitute, cultural background, behavior, or story. Nor could generalizations be made about drug use, child abuse, or even economic need.[12]

Until now, no studies on male prostitution have been published in Costa Rica. Male prostitution, like female prostitution, is not considered a crime, unless it is practiced in a "scandalous" manner. Neither is homosexuality, which ceased to be a crime in the Penal Code of 1971. Before these reforms were introduced, the punishment for sodomy was one to three years in prison (article 233). Since 1971, there has been no basis for the prosecution of homosexuality, as long as it occurs between two consenting adults and passive participants are more than seventeen years of age.[13] However, there are strict laws against pimping (owning a brothel) and inducing minors to practice prostitution. Most convictions are for these two reasons. In order to prosecute an adult prostitute, there must be some other infraction such as moral indecency, public scandal, suspicion of drugs, or vagrancy.[14] Unlike female prostitutes, male prostitutes are not regulated by law, nor are they required to be tested for venereal diseases.

This project does not pretend to be an exhaustive study of male prostitution in Costa Rica. As in the United Kingdom, male prostitution is diverse. There are cheap, middle-class, and high-class centers of prostitution. Brothels range from houses with boys offering the same services as in ancient times to luxurious saunas where massages are given. There is both homosexual and heterosexual prostitution for male and female clients, who may be homosexual, bisexual, or heterosexual. There are also men who perform erotic dances for women, known as *maripepinos* (strippers). Besides dancing, many of them prostitute themselves with their clients. Prostitution is also practiced in saunas, bars, discotheques, hotels, and private homes. Prostitutes may work part-time or full-time. Some do it to earn extra cash or to pay for their university tuition. Others work to buy homes and luxury cars.

This study, however, focuses on a very specific sexual culture within the realm of male prostitution: the young men of a lower-middle-class brothel catering to pederasts. These youths are neither homosexual nor bisexual in the sense of being attracted to both men and women.

How, then, is sexual identity determined? Are these men homosexual, bisexual, or heterosexual? There is no simple answer. Some researchers on sexuality subscribe to the thesis that a bisexual person is one who has sexual relations with both men and women. This idea is shared by Churchill, [15] and Kinsey, Martin, and Gebhard,[16] who define bisexuality as a sexual practice. Other researchers feel that a bisexual person has additional characteristics and cannot be defined by sexual practice alone. Among the criteria that they consider are desire, or the level of attraction toward people of both sexes, as noted by Blumstein and Shwartz,[17] and self-definition, or the personal acceptance of one's sexual identity, according to Warren.[18] Others believe that bisexuality should instead be defined by a "dual affective preference," that is, the desire to have sexual relations with both men and women, and that actual sexual contact should not be interpreted as a "sine qua non" condition.[19-22]

Klein[23] designed a more complex model of bisexuality that includes not only sexual practices and attraction, but also an individual's sexual fantasies, emotional preferences, self-identity, and heterosexual or homosexual lifestyle. Bisexuality is also seen as a variable over time and not as something static, defined by just one characteristic.

In our case study, the young men did not appear to fit into the more complex models of bisexuality; they are not sexually attracted to both sexes, they do not have a bisexual past, they do not have common bisexual fantasies, they do not define themselves as bi-sexuals (although they use the word), they do not have dual emotional relationships, and they do not participate in the homosexual or bisexual lifestyle. The only characteristic that identifies them as bisexual is their sexual behavior. We could say that *cacheros* are only bisexual in terms of their practices, but heterosexual in all other respects.

This contrast between desire and practice places them within a culture known as *cachera*—men who have sexual relations with other men, but who are heterosexual in all other respects.[24] These young men are not from marginal or extremely poor areas. They belong to the lower middle class. Some are students or professionals and some still live with their families, while others have moved into their own homes.

There are many kinds of *cacheros,* but the group studied here is made up of young prostitutes. Not all cacheros are young, and not all prostitutes are *cacheros. Cacherismo* includes mature men who prostitute themselves, prisoners who seek out young or effeminate men and those who are fascinated by transvestites or homosexuals—whether effeminate or not. It also includes many other groups of men in search of female substitutes in different environments or contexts, such as coastal areas, banana-growing zones, the police forces, agricultural areas, and other places where there are not many women. The common denominator of the *cacheros* is that they are men who lead heterosexual lives, but who occasionally have sex with other men, be it for pleasure or for money.

Thus, the group studied here is one of many within the culture of male prostitution and *cacherismo.* This study was carried out in one of the many centers of prostitution that exist in San José. This particular house catered to pederasts, or men attracted to boys and young men, who represent a very specific group within the diverse sexual culture of male prostitution. For this reason, the interviewees are between thirteen and twenty-seven years of age.

Our objective in this study was to learn about the culture of juvenile prostitution with the aim of implementing an immediate intervention program. The young men interviewed are in serious danger of being exposed to the AIDS virus and of becoming addicted—if they are not already—to cocaine, crack, or alcohol. Since prostitution of minors is illegal in Costa Rica, we could have reported the brothel to the authorities. However, this would have been even more counterproductive, since there are many other options available to them, and we would have lost sight of them. Instead, we decided that it was far better to initiate a campaign to supply condoms and raise the young men's awareness about AIDS and drugs, and to begin an immediate support program. This project resulted in the establishment, in June 1997, of an alternative home for juvenile prostitutes, offering various opportunities for education and work.

Since many studies have already demystified the profile of the sex worker, and we have no wish to repeat studies about a hypothetical common background and personality among prostitutes—a phenomenon that has not yet been proven—we have instead chosen to answer some very different questions:

- What is the sexual discourse of men who are masculine, who are attracted to women, and who sell themselves to other men?
- Are there factors that lead to contradictions between discourse and sexual practice?
- What type of sexual culture emerges as a result of these contradictions?

This study was carried out with the help of Antonio Bustamante, MSc, researcher and educator at the Instituto Latinoamericano de Prevención y Educación en Salud (ILPES), with vast experience in the study of *cacherismo* in Central American prisons. Bustamante made the initial contacts and paved the way for our entry into the brothel.

For the purposes of this study, twenty-five young men between the ages of thirteen and twenty-seven were interviewed in one male brothel in San José, Costa Rica. Very few actually live on the premises. The majority of them only show up at night in search of customers. Two interviewers, both members of ILPES, conducted the interviews over a period of six months, from January to June of 1997. The interviews lasted from half an hour to an hour and a half and were carried out privately on the premises. Each young man was paid 1,000 colones (approximately $5) for a half-hour interview, and 5,000 ($25) for hour-and-a-half interviews. The interviewers used a guide consisting of open-ended questions dealing with such issues as sexual initiation, sexual definition, sexual orientation, love, drug use, prostitution, family relationships, and relationships with men and women. Some men were interviewed more than once. The sessions were recorded and later transcribed with a code to prevent identification of the young men or the brothel owner. In addition, four group sessions were held to analyze general topics. The names in this study have been changed to protect the privacy of the participants. Finally, the interviews were transferred to a database known as SAPAC, developed by ILPES for sorting and analysis.

In order to carry out the interviews, we obtained permission from the brothel owner, who was assured that the intention of the study was to understand the situation of heterosexuals involved in male prostitution with the aim of implementing a support project. Given that pimping is a serious crime in this country, and that many of the prostitutes were under eighteen (the legal age for sexual consent), the brothel owner was promised complete confidentiality.

Two gay men participated in the study. One was an acquaintance of the brothel owner, which made the latter more willing to participate in the study. The other introduced himself as a gay man who was merely interested in writing an article to be sent abroad so that others could know and understand the reality of male prostitution. The only condition requested of the owner was the opportunity to conduct the interviews in private. He was also persuaded to immediately accept a free supply of condoms for the prostitutes.

The fact that the interviews were conducted by gay men must be taken into account in analyzing some of the young men's expressed views on homosexuals. If the interviewers had been heterosexual men or women, their responses would most probably have taken a less friendly tone toward homosexuality.

Chapter 1

The House and the Money

THE HOUSE

Lila's house was built in the 1920s as part of a working-class housing project. It is located in a marginal neighborhood in the southern part of San José, Costa Rica. It is surrounded by bars and small businesses. The front of the building is dominated by a peeling and dented door. The handle of the small metal gate has been broken for years. The number plate above the door reads "13-28." As you enter, you see a long, narrow hallway, about four feet wide and nearly forty feet long, with a high ceiling. "This is Sin Alley," says the boy who answers the door.

The designs on the floor tiles contrast with the sawdust, excrement, and dog urine that is everywhere. A wooden three-seater bench is positioned about six feet from the door. "This is my bed sometimes," Lila, the brothel owner, tells us. The first room is about twelve feet from the entrance, on the left-hand side. It is a medium-sized room about fourteen feet long and almost as wide. A naked light bulb hangs from the ceiling and the walls are decorated with tourism posters and a full-length mirror. A dimmer switch controls the light. "It's better not to have too much light," says Mike, a prostitute. "You get some really scary-looking old dudes in here."

The double bed in this first room is placed against the wall and is covered with a torn, stained sheet, made from the same material as the curtain that covers the closed window. Lila and his companion sleep in this bed, which is also used by him and his clientele as a "landing strip," a bed on which sexual relations take place. One of the five large dogs that live in the house occasionally sleeps there as well. "The bed of sin, take a good look," says Lila. "Here, the sheets are witnesses to lust, licentiousness, the weakness of the flesh. . . ."

Near the bed there is a table, approximately five feet long and eighteen inches wide, painted black, with several cigarette burns and what appear to be oil stains. A three-piece moon-shaped mirror set hangs above the table, and on it are a roll of toilet paper, some moisturizing cream, a bottle of rubbing alcohol, some condoms, and a fan. There is a penetrating organic odor: sweat, semen, Sanipine (a disinfectant), and used toilet paper on the floor. Behind the head-board hangs an old green velvet theater curtain. "This was a gift from the deceased Macha," says Lila, "so the neighbors can't make peep holes. It's a very powerful curtain. Macha was a witch."

One of the customers tells us that "here they do three to six hits (sexual encounters) a day, depending what day it is." Jesus, a sex worker, explains that the sheet is changed "every week or two." According to him, "a clean bedspread is used for special clients." This means that the sheet is normally used for around fifty sexual encounters before being washed. According to Lila, use of the room is irregular but frequent. "There are nights when customers knock on the door in the middle of the night and I have to get out of bed to go sleep on the bench in the hall; it's been tough lately, I have no choice." On a busy night, the brothel owner, his companion, and the dog have to leave the room several times to sleep on the bench.

Farther down the hall, which widens slightly, is a small interior garden with flower pots and plastic buckets containing ornamental plants, some hanging from the roof, others from the wall. There is also a white porcelain toilet tank. According to Lila, "the mother-in-law's tongues that I planted in here are to bring in money." Parts of the wall and roof have deteriorated, leaving some areas exposed to the elements. This has benefited the plants, judging by their vigorous growth. "The collapsed wall and the holes in the roof help to get rid of the smells in the house," Lila remarks. "That's wishful thinking—you'd need a whole forest to counteract the smell of dog shit," says Aguilucho, a young prostitute.

There are some huge river boulders surrounded by flower pots. "This rock," explains Lila, "I stole it in the middle of the night, with the help of a couple guys. I'd been seeing it in the same place for years. I liked it so I took it." Mike, one of the boys, cannot see the point in stealing a rock "as if it were a diamond." Every plant, stone, or decorative object has its own story, and Lila is willing to tell them all in intricate detail. Some are his own psychotic fantasies. However, we preferred not to ask, as he tends to talk endlessly and the house is filled with old trinkets.

The kitchen serves as the focal point and meeting place of the house. It measures about twelve feet by ten feet, and is separated from the garden by a wooden folding screen made from woven strips of a beautiful wood that is no longer available in the country. There is a long, narrow table with three plastic chairs, a gas hotplate with four burners, and several cupboards containing a variety of items scattered around: empty bottles, figurines, porcelain and glass vases, some ornamental plants, old newspapers, and a pink hamster cage. This pet, one of Lila's newest acquisitions, runs neurotically on its treadmill. On top of the new white refrigerator sits a German radio from the 1940s, which nearly always plays salsa music. The floor is made of cement and is painted red. Pedro, a customer, disdainfully remarks that "Something's always cooking here. Lila spends everything on feeding the dogs and the punks who hang out here day and night. Everything goes to feed those lazy bums."

The kitchen leads to two rooms. One is the dogs' room, where two large black dogs have lived for the past four years. Sometimes, if they hear a noise, they try to get out, pushing on the door and barking menacingly. The customers and the prostitutes generally become alarmed, whereupon Lila screams at the top of his lungs, "Shut up you sons of bitches. That's enough!" while he pounds on the door with a heavy chain. This routine is repeated four or five times a night.

The dogs are a forbidden topic. Any reference to the foul odors, filth, parasites, or to alleged abuse of the dogs, Lila takes as a personal insult. His reactions to such comments are explosive and aggressive. Don Pedro, a customer, agrees: "I've seen Lila yell and threaten more than one of these guys when they criticize the dogs." According to Lila, the smells and the excrement protect him from possible police raids. "No cop is going to climb over so much shit," he assures us. He certainly has a point: to enter the house, you need to be good at playing hopscotch. One false step could be deadly.

Two of the most vicious dogs eat, urinate, and defecate in this twelve-foot square room. They have no choice but to spend their lives locked up. Salomon, one of the boys, tells us that "Two of the dogs haven't been out for four years. Once in a while he takes the other three for a walk at night." Mike, another one of the boys, thinks that "It's not the police who will raid us, but the health department." Other animals, including rats, mice, cockroaches, and other insects are found throughout the house. The dogs' room is also where the owner keeps his clothing and valuables. Salomon tells us that only Lila can go in this room. "One day I went into the room, and one of the dogs bit me—I still have the scar. I felt betrayed. I hate that dog!" "La Rubia" (the Blond One), a customer, agrees with Mike: "Those dogs have been the ruin of this house. This fool spends over 20,000 colones a month on them." The cockroaches and the mice, however, are more mobile. "I was bent down having oral sex with a guy," recalls a North American client, "when I saw a parade of mice and cockroaches. First, one cockroach went by, and then another, and another. Then the mice came out. Three of them in line, one behind the other. The last one stayed for a few seconds to see what I was doing, so I asked him, 'Could I have a little privacy, please?'"

Lila defends himself from his critics. "If I have to bury myself alive in this house with the dogs, then I'll do it. I'm not going to get rid of them just because some son-of-a-bitch queen criticizes me. I've spent millions on them over these last seven years. What these queens want is to see me ruined, in jail. They're all jealous because I was beautiful and because I like luxury and nice things. They can all go to hell! These dogs love me, they're the only ones who love me. . . . These animals protect me, they're my destiny." Lila continues, "Twenty or twenty-five years ago the deceased Flores predicted it: 'I see you surrounded by eight black dogs that will protect you.'"

The other room leading off from the kitchen is fourteen feet long and about ten feet wide. A single bed takes up most of the space. An old closet with beveled mirrors allows just enough room to pass by. A new electric stove covered with a white sheet fills the rest of the space. According to Lila, "This stove was given to me by a gringo who fell in love with Mike." For years, this room has been rented or reserved for "emergencies." Now it is occupied by Hector, also known as "Rambo," a masculine, muscular, good-looking twenty-two-year-old sex worker. According to Lila, Hector is the one who is most sought after by the clients: he will do anything, and almost does it for love. However, Lila bemoans the fact that "He's so strange; he doesn't talk. I think he's sick. He treats me very badly, he insults me, he doesn't respect me; I keep him here because I feel sorry for him. He goes to bed at five in the morning after whoring all night. He gets up at six in the evening. He doesn't help me with anything; he doesn't even want to wash the dogs. Too bad he's so weird. With a body and a dick like that, he should be a millionaire, but no, he just wants to whore and sleep. He's very strange." "Rambo" himself confirms that "I've had up to five customers a day. I'll take anything, whatever it is."

According to Lila, "La Montaña" and his lover, Quique, used to live in Rambo's room. "La Montaña got this room when he was fifteen. Mike also used to live there, with his squeeze, 'til the stupid slut got pregnant and I threw them both out. I loved him dearly, and I still do, but he was destroying me little by little. You can't live with a hardened player."

Separated from the dining room by a wooden screen, the kitchen sink is located in a space two and a half meters by two meters. It is a damp, dirty-looking place. The lower part of the wall has caved in and is exposed to the elements. You can see the patio of the house next door (which has been closed off for the past year). Sewage flows freely underneath the sink. The water is so foul that seven puppies from the last litter who drank some died of poisoning. During the rainy season, water pours onto the floor through the holes in the roof. Next to the sink there are some unpainted wooden shelves, worn by water and time. Various kitchen utensils sit on the shelves. Occasionally, small rats scamper across them. You can hear the sound of the rodents' offspring. Lila explains that "I don't kill rats because they, too, are parents and have the right to live. They'll go away someday. . . . " This doesn't seem very likely in the near future. "The rats are happy at Lila's. They feel welcomed and appreciated," says Pedro. "They don't even hide," he says.

Next to the washroom is the bathroom. A piece of cloth held in place with tacks serves as a door. The bathroom is small, four feet wide and about seven feet long. Neither the sink nor the toilet works properly. A North American client visiting the house for the first time comments, "Jesus Christ! After doing my thing with the guy, I went to the sink to use some mouthwash. I gargled, spat into the sink, and—ah, it was so gross—the mouthwash spilled directly onto my new sneakers! There was no pipe—I could see right down through the sink to my shoes!"

The shower has no curtain. The prostitutes bathe here, as do some of the clients. Lila also uses the shower to wash out the rag he constantly uses to mop up the dogs' urine. Small shelves display empty flowerpots and bottles of medicine and liquor, some of which are broken or have not been touched for years. There are also tubes of toothpaste and disposable razors. A vine that dried up years ago is still planted and stuck to the wall. There is an empty fishbowl. The dogs drink from the toilet bowl.

Next to the bathroom is a tiny five foot square patio, a kind of utility room with no door. Nearby, there is a large new white washing machine. According to Lila, it was given to him by a client "who wanted to win me over."

The largest space is the living room, which is around fourteen feet wide by eighteen feet long. An altar to Saint Barbara, decorated by a client and friend, occupies the position of honor—a six-foot long, eighteen-inch-wide platform that stands about three feet high. The platform is draped with red velvet. An enclosure of pink and magenta feathers covers the nine-inch-high statuette of the saint. The owner says the statuette was given to him by "La Duquesa" (The Duchess), a guy who came from France and who "had powers." "I admire St. Barbara," says Lila, "because she was a princess who chose to die rather than be humiliated. They say her own father cut off her tits." The statue is surrounded with magical accessories: a pack of Spanish cards that Lila uses in his reading sessions, a bronze goblet, an oil lamp that burns twenty-four hours a day, fruits, and red ornaments. There is a picture of the Afro-Caribbean deity Changó. "It was given to me by a Cuban friend who painted it himself." A white card with the Hebrew character Aleph printed in red is used for offerings, and there is also a bell made of bronze and wood. Another dog sleeps under the altar. Occasionally, incense is burned. When times are hard, Lila prays and meditates in front of the altar. Sometimes, he cries. According to Mike, "The day after a Cuban sorcerer 'cleaned' the place up, I saw him cry like a baby. He was kneeling and the Cuban put his arms around him."

On the other side of the living room there is a small unused bar upon which the Christmas Nativity scene is built. The brothel owner admits that the scene "is famous throughout the neighborhood." The Nativity scene is displayed in December, to coincide with St. Barbara's feast day. It is taken down in April, after Easter Week and after a rosary has been said. Parts of the floor have come loose where the ground has sunk and the tiles have not been put back in place.

Two large fishbowls shed a faint, greenish light. A bubbling sound can be heard, though there are no oxygen pumps. One day we saw Lila transferring a fish from one tank to the other. "Come here, baby. Keep still! Come to Mama. Don't jump, you son of a bitch. I'm the boss here!" he said to one of the large golden carp. The fish died a few days later. It floated for hours before anyone bothered to take it out. "This fish here," says Lila, "cost me around seven thousand colones. I've spent a fortune on them. They're more grateful than the bastards who live here, who don't give a shit. I feed them Japanese food that costs me 1,500 colones a day."

In one corner of the living room there is a narrow door secured by a thin chain. It leads to the last room in the house, known as the "landing strip." It was originally a kitchen, but for years this room has been rented or used by itinerant young men, many of whom do "extra" work in the house. The room is ten feet long and eight feet wide. It has a single bed, and Lila has put a table on top of the old wash sink, using it as a place to pile his shirts. The current occupant, Cesar, hangs his clothes on a metal rod. He has decorated the room with photographs and posters of girls in swim suits. A well-known picture of Marilyn Monroe hangs on the grey discolored door. "If this room could talk . . ." Salomon remarks. Quique adds, "A very drunk, drugged-up client tried to strangle me here one day. Lila saved me when he heard my screams." Raul, a client, recalls that one day in this room "Two kids pulled a gun on me and threatened to kill me. In the end I talked them into selling me the gun. Then I beat them both up."

Lila has his own story about this room. "One day, during a fight, someone tried to rob me and they locked me in here, and I broke my hand trying to get out through the ceiling. I almost killed myself, but I landed like a feather." Lola, a friend, says that in this room, "I scratched the son of a bitch who lived here in the face, and I left marks—nobody makes a fool of me." Aguilucho, one of the young men who has worked longest at the house, lights a joint and comments, "The only room in this house that's kept neat is this one."

In recent months, the room has been used as an office to conduct interviews and as a bedroom for Cesar, a twenty-one-year-old sex worker. He recently moved here because of family problems. His girlfriend visits him often and they lock themselves in the room. Cesar charges at least 3,000 colones for sex without penetration. "No son of a bitch is going to touch my ass. If the client wants penetration, he's got to give me a toucan (5,000-colon bill)." He says his girlfriend does not know "that this is a whorehouse or that I work here because she's never taken a look to see what's going on in the landing strip."

THE CLIENTS

They creep into the house stealthily and leave even more quickly. They choose the guy they like and go into a room. It seems that they do not exist because you hardly see them. "It's not that people are scared at Lila's. It's just that it's swarming with ghosts," says Mike. If you listen carefully, you can just make out sighs, barely suppressed exclamations of pleasure, a little groan of pain. "They've nailed [penetrated, in jargon] the Venezuelan!" Lila says softly. "When you have experience as a madam," he continues, "you get to know what goes on behind closed doors." As we paid more attention, it seemed that he was right: the Venezuelan was moaning with pleasure. "However," he added, "one day I was wrong. They were strangling a queen and I just thought he was coming. Sometimes it's hard to tell the difference between orgasm and strangulation." A few minutes later, the Venezuelan came out. He did not greet us, or look at us, or say anything: he simply went out onto the street and disappeared into the night. "That queen's a journalist," said Lila, "and look how she moves her ass."

Who are the clients? What kind of men come to a place like this? They are not generally willing to be seen or interviewed. "No, no!" exclaimed Lila. "Are you crazy, wanting to interview my clients? I'll be run out of business." Neither the owner nor the prostitutes wanted the clients to be interviewed. "If we let you talk to them, tomorrow you'll be bringing Pilar Cisneros[1] with her TV cameras. Then, you guys will be on Cristina's show,[2] while I'm rotting in jail for pimping," said the brothel owner. "The only way to get a closer look at them is to ask the prostitutes," he suggested as a compromise. "Next they're going to ask me if they can film a fuck!" said Lila to Mike, in a tone of exasperation and uneasiness.

There are many types of "regular" clients at this place. Most of them are interested in young men ages fifteen to twenty. Others, a minority, prefer boys ages ten to fourteen years. Yet another group has no age preference; they come here because men are available and they can even choose thirty-five-year-olds. Gerardo, a soccer referee, works from time to time at the house. "I've got more energy and experience than any shithead around here. Look at this body," he tells us. "Isn't it sexy?" However, his type is not the "specialty of the house." Lila's brothel is best known as a place for pederasts and pimps. "Our clients like youth. There are other houses for old *cacheros*," says Mike.

Unlike the prostitutes, the clients' sexual orientation is bisexual. Most of them are married men with children, who are completely "in the closet," as Lila says. In other words, these men lead a heterosexual life in public, with occasional visits to the brothel. Nevertheless, there are also some homosexuals among the clients. However, as we will see below, the prostitutes do not like homosexual clients. "They're never satisfied. They always want more and more sex, they want you to kiss them on the mouth and say things to them. They're a pain in the ass. I'd rather not go with them, so I concentrate on the *viejos* [mature men]," says Cerebró, a prostitute. For *cacheros*, homosexuals are generally effeminate men who move within the gay community, live with other men, and have not married or had children. The *viejos* are those who hide their homosexuality well, who are masculine, and whom one would never suspect of being homosexual.

Although bisexual clients appear to be masculine, there are significant differences—besides age—between themselves and the sex workers. One of them is desire. Paying clients express feelings of sexual attraction for other men, enjoy sexual relations, and began their secret homosexual lives years ago. "Clients like what's done to them—if not, they wouldn't pay," says Hugo. "You can tell they like gay sex," says Mono. According to Lila, many of his clients have been coming for more than twenty years and started young. One of the few clients that we were able to interview, "El Flaco" (the Thin Man), confesses that he started paying men for sex when he was seventeen years old. Now, age thirty-nine, he admits he enjoys it just as much: "I'm married and have children. I do this once a month when my hormones flare up."

Bisexual clients also differ from homosexual clients. Bisexuals are more attracted by the prostitutes' youth, while homosexuals are attracted by their masculinity. Mono explains why:

> The homosexuals who come here are looking for a man. What attracts them is not youth, but masculinity. In gay bars, there are masculine homosexuals but they are a minority. The younger "fairies" who want to feel like women come to be penetrated. When you're with them, they act and talk so much like women that you feel like you're in a hen house. Some guys like them because it's like being with a woman. Others hate them for being effeminate. The masculine clients, on the other hand, are respectable family men, some are even grandfathers.

In terms of sexual practice, there is also great variety. Cerebrón prefers older customers because "they treat you more like a son" and "They help you more, they don't beat around the bush, and if you need something they give it to you because they know they're old. They're not so interested in sodomy." Hugo agrees that clients who are married and have relations with women "are different from homosexuals. They're not so demanding." However, he believes they are interested in penetration. Erick does not think there is a general pattern for any single client. "Each guy has a different relationship with a client. With some, the client may be active, and with others, passive. With me, El Flaco is extremely passive even though he's married and 'macho.' With others he may be active, I don't know." There are also some very effeminate homosexuals who are active. "La Preciada is active despite being a complete woman," says Mono. "Life's full of surprises," replies Lila, and adds, "You can't kid yourself and keep on believing that a married, masculine man is necessarily active. I've seen thousands of 'macho men' who, instead of attacking and dominating you, get down on all fours. If I see that a man is not going to dominate me, then I dominate him and fuck him. I'm a queer, but I'm not a coward."

Many of the prostitutes believe that clients have trouble picking up sex partners because of their age, looks, or weight. Cerebrón comment, "If they had pretty faces, they wouldn't be here." He says many of them are so fat that "You can't even see their dick because of their stomach." The man with the glasses has "such a big belly that he looks like he's eight months pregnant," adds Luis. But others say that it's not only ugly men who frequent the place. "No way!" says Mono. "We get good-looking guys who could have any man or woman they wanted, but they don't because they don't want to get a reputation, so they come here because it's quick and discreet." The owner agrees: "We get everything. I've got clients who ask about other clients . . . they want to take them into a room, because they're so good."

The clients' social status is equally varied. Although Lila's house leaves much to be desired, and the dirt has driven away many customers, he still receives middle-class and wealthy clients. This is what Hugo has to say:

> What we get is working middle-class people—some are professors, others are bar owners. There are others who are real upper crust—there are two really rich guys here. One is very arrogant and thinks he owns the world. The other one isn't like that, he treats people well.

One of the rich men who frequents the brothel is the famous and mysterious "El Conde" (the Count). He pays the rent of the house in exchange for complete discretion and absolute confidentiality. "The Count," says Mike, "is someone hardly anyone knows except us. The owner throws everyone out of the house when he's expected. He's a very rich and important man. His turn-on is watching erotic scenes involving several guys. When he comes here, Lila chooses the best guys to treat him like a king. He's a fat man with glasses. I've seen him, and people would die if they knew who he was." "Can we find out who the Count is?" we asked Lila. "Sure, I'd be happy to tell you," he replied, "if you give me your credit card number and a blank check. Can't you see that if I open my mouth, I'll end up with my tongue in the fish tank—and maybe yours, too?"

Although there are rich clients, most are from modest backgrounds. Lila's house is cheaper than many other brothels. The price of a "hit" is less than ten thousand colones, including room and prostitute. In saunas where prostitution is practiced, the cost of the masseur and the room are double. "People are throwing their money away when they go to those saunas. I'm telling you, Lila's is cheaper and you pay half as much. 'Listen, you fools,' I say, 'don't you see that here you can save ten thousand colones for the same thing?'" Despite Cerebrón's sales pitch, the saunas are cleaner, and many middle-class men prefer them.

Although, as we shall see later, emotional relationships develop between clients and prostitutes, the transaction can also be crude and commercial. Adults regard these young men as sexual objects, and there is minimal conversation.

1st Interviewer:	What is it that attracts clients here?
Hugo:	What most clients are looking for is a big dick.

Cerebrón agrees:

1st Interviewer:	Do clients propose marriage to you?
Cerebrón:	Yeah, lots.
1st Interviewer:	Why do you think that happens?
Cerebrón:	I don't know—must be because of my dick. I have a bunch of clients who are in love with it.
1st Interviewer:	And that doesn't bother you?
Cerebrón:	No, actually I feel proud.
1st Interviewer:	But wouldn't you rather that they fell in love with you for your mind?
Cerebrón:	Of course! But most of them are queers, and since they're so interested in dicks . . .

Hugo tells us that clients are interested in a big penis, "like a horse." When we asked him if some of the guys have been rejected for being less well-endowed, he said, "No, not very often. However, clients discuss all our characteristics among themselves. Maybe the first time they'll go with someone small, but the next time they'll look for the biggest one."

Other requests from clients, such as sadomasochism, are often turned down. Luis says he "hates it" when they ask him to use vibrators or alcohol. "Some of them ask me to use alcohol. Do you have any idea how much that hurts?" Others like pain or scratching and biting, "things that really bother me." Hugo has had violent scenes with clients: "One day I was with a guy from Puriscal and we went to his house. I was joking and asked him if he liked to give his ass. He had a record in his hand, and he threw it down, slapped me, threatened me, and treated me like a dog."

Some prostitutes take revenge on their clients by robbing them. If someone picks them up in a public place (not at Lila's or in a sauna) and is loaded with money, as Cerebrón says, he's setting himself up to be robbed. According to Cerebrón, clients who go to bars and come out drunk run the risk that "the guys will leave them naked in the street." He explains how and why he robs some of his clients:

2nd Interviewer:	OK, so can we conclude that besides the money that clients pay you for sex, you also have the opportunity to rob them?
Cerebrón:	Yeah, but let's say you and I go to a hotel, or where there's nobody nearby, we do it, and then after it's over you tell me that you don't have much money, you take out your wallet and I see lots of toucans [5,000-colon bills], but you only give me 3,000. That's when I'd rob you.
2nd Interviewer:	How do you do it?
Cerebrón:	You say, "Give me your money," and you take out the knife, and if he doesn't cooperate, you grab him and shove him up against the wall. You don't need a knife to scare people.
2nd Interviewer:	Just by looking mean?

Cerebrón:	Yeah, just by looking mean, pure acting.
2nd Interviewer:	So I suppose that means you have to be careful and size up the kind of client you pick up. You don't pick a heavy guy?
Cerebrón:	No, because I'm not going to pick up someone who will sock me in the mouth.
2nd Interviewer:	Have you ever attacked anyone?
Cerebrón:	There's no need to make a scene. If you pull a knife on someone and cut them just a little, they back off.
2nd Interviewer:	Do you have the knife on you now?
Cerebrón:	No, it's hidden in the park.
2nd Interviewer:	And if a client turns up here?
Cerebrón:	No, I don't rob anyone here in the house. I attack people on the street, or I take the client somewhere else and tell him that we're going to a friend's apartment, but before we reach the house, he's up against the wall.

Despite the potential for violence, most transactions between *cacheros* and clients pass off without incident. "It's better to make money without having to rob people, because if you're known as a thief no one will want you afterwards," confesses Cerebrón.

Since we were unable to interview clients, it is difficult to speculate about what attracts them to prostitutes and why they take risks with *cacheros*. However, in an earlier study on men who pick up other men in public places, interviewees confessed that they found dangerous sex with hookers and possible assailants "exciting" and "addictive." Many of the men who regularly visit a park in San José to pick up other men have been mugged or even stabbed. However, despite the risks, they continue to frequent these dangerous places.[3]

One may speculate that clients and *cacheros* are both addicted, although their addictions differ. The prostitutes are generally addicted to money and drugs, while their clients are addicted to dangerous or kinky sex. The combination of these two complementary addictions is explosive.

CACHEROS

The young men who work at Lila's house are, with a few exceptions, between ten and twenty-five years of age. Most of them are from the local neighborhood, though some come from areas farther away. This fact is important, because the only reason for establishing the brothel in this particular place was the low rent. Lila did not choose a particular neighborhood, and indeed, could have chosen any other lower-middle-class area of San José. "You can find young men willing to prostitute themselves anywhere in the country," he says.

These *cacheros,* then, share certain characteristics with other lower-middle-class youths: they have homes, basic electronic gadgets, television, and opportunities for education and recreation. The majority are not street kids from marginal areas, nor do they have half-caste features. They are generally attractive, some are blond and blue-eyed, and some are well-dressed. Their conversation reflects their exposure to the media and an awareness of current events. Some are high school or university students. Others have had little formal education, yet are well-informed and intelligent. Mono, for example, is an avid reader who talks like a college student and displays sharp critical faculties. In some of the interviews, he ended up asking his own questions and anticipating the direction of the interview.

However, other aspects of their backgrounds are more in keeping with the image of the stereotypical prostitute: the young men do not know their fathers or have bad relationships with them; they have been thrown out of their homes; they have a family history of alcoholism, a criminal record, have been victims of child abuse or have seen their mothers abused. Cerebrón was abandoned by his mother, and was eventually raised by his alcoholic grandmother. Jonás, whose mother is a prostitute, was also raised by his grandparents. Carlos was brutally beaten by his father. Luis was thrown out onto the streets when he began taking drugs and never returned home.

However, these difficult past experiences should not lead us to conclude that prostitution is the result of poverty and broken homes. In fact, the young men interviewed here are typical of their environment. Absentee fathers are common in a country where almost 50 percent of households are headed by women. Alcoholism affects 30 percent of Costa Rican households. Crack is consumed by large sectors of the population. Violence is endemic in the country. Thirty percent of university students have been victims of incest. Most children were neither planned nor wanted.[4] If these conditions, in themselves, were the causes of prostitution, there would be hundreds of thousands of young prostitutes.

Some of the *cacheros* come from "normal" homes. Erick lives with his parents, who work for a public institution and do not have the slightest idea that their son is a prostitute. Gerardo is a very respectable middle-class soccer referee with a good job and a family. Mario has a good relationship with his parents. Ernesto's parents are Christians, and at his home you never hear so much as a bad word.

If we had carried out this study in a middle- or high-class sauna, we would have found the same thing: young men who are representative of their backgrounds. Prostitution among the rich is perhaps more sophisticated than among the poor. There are boys from very good homes who prostitute themselves for pleasure or to satisfy certain needs, or to avoid asking their parents for money. They would be more discreet and would probably rely on certain connections for their "contacts." Nevertheless, they would still be offering sex for money.

The stereotype of the prostitute serves a social function: it makes us believe that if we could find solutions to poverty and broken homes, we would eliminate prostitution. Conservative and religious groups utilize this idea to impose their vision of families obedient to Church and State as an antidote to "social evils." The same happens with the fight against drugs, which is invariably linked to prostitution. Although it is true that drugs increase dependency on prostitution, we cannot say that there is a cause-and-effect relationship between the two. Gerardo is a prostitute and does not take drugs. Mario became a prostitute long before he started using crack. Luis does not drink, and has never even smoked a cigarette.

We may speculate that the link between drugs and prostitution is established in other ways: through religious guilt and discrimination against prostitutes. If they were seen as regular workers, they would have more self-esteem and less need to dull their pain through the use of alcohol, barbiturates, video games, cigarettes, marijuana, crack, money, cards, and, of course, sex. If they were not compelled to hide like criminals, they would behave less like criminals. This is precisely Mono's viewpoint:

> I believe one becomes a degenerate because only degenerates accept prostitution. If people respected us for the work we do, instead of denigrating it, we would associate with other people and would even have the opportunity to form a union.

THE BROTHEL OWNER

"I'm Cleopatra, I'm Eva Perón—that's how I want to be remembered," says Lila. "Is that how you'd like us to begin the section on you?" we asked him. "No, I'm not Eva Perón or Cleopatra, though I've always admired them." Instead of Egypt or Argentina, Lila tells us he was born in Naranjo de Alajuela to a prostitute mother and an absentee father. He was one of twelve siblings fathered by different men. "My mother told me that she wasn't a prostitute, but said she lived with various men in order to support herself and maintain her family," Lila says sadly. As soon as he was born, he was given away. "Mama gave me up because she was sick . . . she had an illness that women don't recover from." We asked him what it was, and he told us it was "puerperal fever," an ailment of the vagina for which there was no cure in 1938. Lila's mother did not actually die from this illness. She made a deal with the doctor, whose mother desperately wanted a child. "The doctor suggested to my mother that she give me to her mother to take care of," he tells us. When the biological mother recovered, her friends convinced her that it was better to leave the child where he was. Lila says his mother's friends would tell her, "Don't be a fool. You're poor and you don't even have a hole to die in, but this family is rich. Leave the kid there."

Like Moses, Lila grew up not knowing his origins. His real mother visited him until he was around five, but to him she was "a domestic employee who came from time to time." However, the local townspeople made sure he discovered his origins. "I found out whose son I was at the age of seven, because in Naranjo they called me 'Son of the Cat, Son of the Cat,' so I discovered the truth. 'The Cat' was a local guy."

His adoptive mother was an "indifferent," "strong," and "strange" woman. When we asked him what he meant by "strange," he explained that she did something to him that "just isn't done." She forbade him to "play," because, according to her, "only lazy bums play." Lila blames his adoptive mother for having turned him into a "very sensitive" and "effeminate" child and for not allowing him to play soccer or other "manly" games. However, he also attributes his femininity to the sexual abuse that he experienced at the hands of an electrician, with whom he had a relationship for seven years. "I started imitating women because this man turned me on and I wanted to attract men the same way women do."

2nd Interviewer:	What happened when you were a child?
Lila:	When I was seven, I went on an errand for my mother. I went to get the electrician, who was a close friend of the family. This guy was very affectionate with me, very charming. He was loving and treated me like the father I never had. We had a great friendship, and I never thought anything about it. But one afternoon, when I was seven and was in church at catechism class, he came to collect me and took me to the movies, which horrified me. I didn't know what a theater was, I didn't know what a screen was . . . I told him I couldn't get home too late because I'd get into trouble, but since I knew that my family liked him, I said, "Well, only if you take me home later," and he said he would. So then I thought, "OK, if he brings me home, I won't get into trouble," and he told me, "This is a very good movie. Your mother won't have any reason to be mad at you. We're going to see a Tarzan movie with giraffes and elephants." And of course, I wanted to see elephants, doves, jungle. He said, "Tell the

teacher you don't feel good, and come with me," so that's what I did. It didn't scare me that this man touched my legs and my face because it was normal and he'd always done this in front of my adoptive mother. I never felt there was any malice in his touching, but that day at the movies, in the middle of the movie, he started touching my legs again, he opened his pants a little, took my hand, put it on his penis, and told me to touch it. I touched it, but what I felt was curiosity because it was so big. He said, "I'm a grown man, and you're a little boy; yours will grow little by little. Touch it, touch it!"

2nd Interviewer: What else happened there?

Lila: Well, I touched his penis. And he touched me, and the relationship continued.

2nd Interviewer: This pattern of touching, how long did it last?

Lila: Seven years.

2nd Interviewer: In other words, from the time you were seven to fourteen years old.

Lila's story gradually began to unfold like Cinderella's. His adoptive mother had her own children and grandchildren who regarded him as an interloper. He was extremely effeminate and his family rejected him. He was made to sweep and clean the house (author's note: the resulting trauma might explain why he never cleans his own house). One day he got into a fight with one of his adoptive mother's granddaughters. She took the radio away from him while he was listening to "Radio Fides," a religious station, his only diversion. "Give me the radio or I'll slap you," Lila threatened, and the girl went running to her grandmother. She told Lila, "You're nobody, you have no rights to anything, you're just someone we picked up." He answered, "If I'm nobody then I'll be free and I'll do what I want." At the age of fifteen, he gathered his things together and left the house. He fled to a friend's farm in Heredia. Here he was offered room and board in exchange for domestic help. "The house was very dirty, but I was already good at cleaning, as I was used to scrubbing floors and walls and washing cars." However, the housemaid fell in love with him. He was by now a handsome young man with green eyes and honey-colored hair. In fact, he was so attractive that the maid practically raped him:

> I could have stayed at this house longer if it hadn't been for the maid. She wanted to seduce me—she started feeding me very well, but I never thought she was going to attack me. She ended up dragging me into bed. I didn't know what to do because I was so scared—I had never been with a woman. I didn't want to give her the satisfaction of saying I was a homosexual, so I did it. This lasted for about three months until one day I fell asleep in her room. The lady of the house came home from Mass, had a fit, and threw me out.

Lila swore that "this would be the last house that I'd be thrown out of," and he headed for the capital. "One day they told me that this woman had given birth to a son with green eyes, who could be my son," he told us, ending this chapter of his life.

Life in San José proved to be very different. He was forced to sleep on the street, and thus began his life of prostitution.

Lila: I had no home in San José, so I had to sleep on the streets. Obviously, the only people who could help me were street gays or some kind-hearted female prostitute. With no home and no friends, I had no choice but to go with men. I had to survive. And worst of all, I was underage and no hotel would rent me a room. I had to beg them to do it.

2nd Interviewer: So, you had two types of friends: homosexuals and clients.

Lila: Yes.

2nd Interviewer: Who were the clients?

Lila: Well, macho types who liked young men but who weren't effeminate. At that time I wasn't considered a homosexual, but rather a *cachero*.

Lila was not very successful. "I was willing to go with a ninety-year-old man or with a twenty-year-old laborer. What I wanted was a good friendship or to live well, but my homosexual friends always bitched about me. All those friends I had, they didn't let me live in peace. If I'd been more masculine, the attraction would have been greater." Later, he began to rent rooms to homosexuals and *cacheros*.

Many homosexuals were jealous of him:

> It makes me furious to hear them talk about how beautiful I was. It makes me so mad because in those days nobody told me that. It's hard to believe, but sometimes ugly people are luckier than good-looking ones. All these friends got in my way or made my life impossible. They spoke badly of me, they wouldn't give me a break, all because I had a beautiful face. I don't think it was my body so much, because I was thin, but what definitely caught people's attention was my face, because it was androgynous.

For fifteen years, Lila worked the streets as a prostitute. He ended up living in a cave near the Virilla River, which he fixed up as a home.

> At that time it was difficult to find someone who would rent a room to a minor. I had a baby face and I never looked my age. In those days, there were [police] raids on sleazy hotels and I was afraid of being caught. Since I bathed and washed my clothes in the Virilla River, I discovered some caves where they had excavated sand, like a quarry. So, to avoid the police raids, I found some refrigerator boxes, and I put one on the ground, and the other against the wall to block out the draft. I slept there from two in the morning until ten. When it warmed up, I washed my clothes, which dried on the river rocks around one in the afternoon, and then I returned to San José by bus for twenty cents.

When he turned thirty-five, Lila met the famous El Conde, who has been his patron and guardian for the last twenty years. With his help, he opened his first house, which, like the present establishment, offered rooms for rent. In the beginning, Lila rented rooms to men who came with friends. Later, the young men were added to his business. Lila insists that he merely introduces these young men to friends and does not prostitute them. "They [the young men] get into this because they want to earn money, and they look for the men themselves. What I did—and do—is simply make introductions, nothing more." In 1973, Lila was brought to trial, after two lesbians accused him of pimping. The women wanted to take revenge because Lila had thrown them out of his house. He was convicted and spent two years in jail (this explains his fear of being taken away again) and then opened a bar for black people, which was later closed down by an evangelist "who objected to black people having a place of their own." In 1988, Lila was again accused of pimping, but was acquitted because of a lack of evidence. "It was a setup by a rich guy who'd killed one of the young men I introduced him to, and who'd been his lover. I knew he was the murderer, so to discredit me, he paid two guys 125,000 colones to testify that I'd raped them in my house." At the time, Lila rented the present house, which he has now occupied for fourteen years.

Many clients and many young men have passed through Lila's house. "In fourteen years, you see a lot of people. Every year you meet many people. Sometimes you see someone you haven't seen in fifteen years. Many young men who have gone abroad come back to visit me. They come with cars and clothes from Fifth Avenue. Others end up dead in a ditch. That's life. Thousands have passed through here." However, Lila's house is as much a refuge for the young as it is a center of prostitution. "I don't close the door to any young person, or demand anything from them in return for a bed. As I told you, I can't stand a boy being thrown out on the street, like I was. Sometimes there are eight guys here, and I feed them all. Many of the rich clients who visit these kids criticize me for giving them food and shelter, but I can't stand to see a boy go hungry."

Is Lila a Sorcerer?

Lila says he possesses magical powers and the ability to read the cards:

> Well, over the years I've realized that I was attracted to, or that I enjoyed reading the cards. It wasn't 'til I was thirty-five that I realized I could do it without having read anything about it.

Maybe it's not my mind, but I cut the deck well, and I find what the person needs to know, what concerns him. I cut the cards, I read them, and it always works out. However, I don't practice this profession because I've always been afraid of God, and the occult belongs more to the Prince of Darkness. I've already made a mess of my life, so I'm not going to get involved in satanic practices.

Lila also believes in the supernatural. He not only reads the cards, but also says he has telepathic and telekinetic powers. Hugo confirms this:

The neighbors are afraid of witchcraft, because Lila really is a sorcerer. He has some sort of telepathic powers, because recently I was at home, and I heard his voice. He touched my shoulder and said, "Hugo, come over here. I have a client." So, I went over to Lila's place and he said, "I was thinking about you. Look, I have a client." And I said to myself, "Son of a bitch! It really was him who was calling me through telepathy!"

Lila has a statue of Changó, one of the gods of the Cuban religious cult known as Santería. Although we never saw him participate in any rituals other than praying for a favor, some people claim that he prepares cures and potions and even casts spells to punish his enemies.

We do not know whether Lila is a sorcerer or whether he has special powers. People believe that on some days, he flies on his broom (which must serve some purpose, since it is certainly not used for sweeping), and on others that he predicts the future, casts spells, or turns some client into a black dog—or even worse, a rat or the hamster in the pink cage. However, it serves his purpose that people believe in his powers, because that way they leave him alone:

Before, the neighbors used to harass Lila. They would call the police and ask them to raid the premises. Some of the parents talked about burning down the house with Lila and everything inside. But they soon backed off when they saw that Lila really was a sorcerer. A very devout Catholic woman had a vision during Holy Week that Lucifer had moved into the neighborhood . . . and he was none other than Lila. A man from the local evangelical church fainted when he passed by the front door of the house. He claimed that a terrible supernatural force had bowled him over right there. A young virgin from the neighborhood didn't bleed at all on her wedding night, and the groom explained that Lila had cast a spell on her. On other occasions, terrible moans that sound like Lucifer himself can be heard coming from one of the rooms. [Author's note: Could they not be the moans of the Venezuelan?] Since these things began happening, no one messes with Lila.

"Lila, are you the devil himself?" we asked. He replied, "Look, I believe in God and Satan. I'm a respectful, God-fearing person. If you do good, He will protect you. Don't you see I could never be a real devil? If I were bad, I'd be a little, second-rate devil. The real demons never got a hold of me; I'm just a speck in the universe of evil."

As researchers, we could not resist an attempt to verify these powers. We asked him to read the cards for us, and predict what would happen with our book. This was his answer:

I see a great scandal on the horizon. Few will understand the reasons for writing this book. Most will criticize you, they will call you sick, they will portray you as degenerates, atheists, perverts. But the book will be a success. People will buy many copies, and the main star, Lila, will be famous. I see stripes, but I don't know if I will end up in jail or dressed in zebra skin.

PROFIT AND MONEY LAUNDERING

Studies on prostitution in England and other places have established that money is the main reason for heterosexual men to practice prostitution.[5] The same phenomenon is also very evident at this brothel—so much so that it does not merit further discussion.

When the *cacheros* were asked about their monthly incomes, it was impossible for them to answer. They are only aware of their daily earnings. Practically none of them had any idea of saving for the future. *Cacheros* live for the moment, and this is reflected in their spending habits and their budget. Two factors make it difficult to pinpoint exactly the amount of their monthly incomes. One of these factors is known as "money laundering." *Cacheros* do not want those closest to them to know the source or amount of their earnings. In this way, they can spend their money on luxuries or on drugs, without having to share it with their families or lovers. The other factor has to do with morality. *Cacheros* regard the money they earn through prostitution as "dirty," and feel it should be spent as quickly as possible to minimize the guilt. As a result, they are only aware of their daily incomes, and spend the money as fast as they earn it.

These young men charge from 1,000 colones (U.S. $5) to 10,000 colones (U.S. $50) for sex. Masturbation is cheapest at 1,000 colones, while active anal sex varies from 2,000 to 5,000 colones, and passive sex costs between 5,000 and 10,000. Given that some *cacheros* service two to eight clients per day, their monthly incomes may range from around 80,000 colones up to more than half a million colones. The majority probably earn around 150,000 per month, which is more than a teacher makes. Since many of them have little formal education, they could only expect to earn one-quarter or even one-tenth of their present incomes as unskilled workers.

Martin, age sixteen, earns a minimal amount from prostitution. He began working at thirteen, and generally prostitutes himself "only when I need money." He says he makes around 5,000 colones a week. Occasionally, he may have sex with up to fifteen clients, but that is unusual, according to him. When asked what he does with the 5,000 colones that he earns, he says he spends the money as follows:

- Food: 2,000 colones
- Clothes: 2,000 colones
- Transportation: 1,000 colones

Martin is a student in his eighth year of high school and lives at home with his parents, six brothers and sisters, his grandparents, and an uncle. Only his parents and his uncle work, which means the family must live on a minimal budget. Although Martin does not have to contribute to the household, there is no money left over for any "luxuries," as he says. One of these luxuries is eating chicken. In his house, they can afford to serve "only rice and beans." Even less money is available to buy clothing, "except what I earn in this business."

Martin has had a girlfriend for the past year, and began having sex with her three months ago. The money he earns through prostitution "runs through my hands like water." He takes his girlfriend to the movies, pays for taxis, and invites her to eat at McDonald's. Since Martin does not receive any spending money from his parents for "luxuries," he picks up his "extras" at Lila's. These "extras" are considered "easy money," money that is "blown" quickly. When we asked him what he considers to be the difference between "easy" and "hard-earned" money, he told us that the former is not "honest" money and is therefore squandered. However, the income from an "exhausting" job, like working ten hours in a supermarket, is saved.

This distinction between "easy" and "honest" money seems to reflect a sense of guilt about working as a prostitute. Martin tells us that he considers the money earned from prostitution to be "dirty money" and that he does it "out of hunger." However, as we have seen, this "hunger" is not for food, but for "luxuries," or the normal things that all kids want. More than guilt or a sense of sin, "easy money" also acquires a magical quality that allows it to be used for luxuries, clothes, watches, music, or good food.

However, "easy money" must be "laundered," or spent quickly, to hide its origin. Martin has no good explanation for where his money comes from. He says his mother "has no idea" what he does for a living. Therefore, he cannot bring the money home, since he would have to explain where it came from. Alberto, who earns several thousand colones per week, is in the same situation. Instead of sharing the money with his younger siblings, he prefers to "keep a little for drugs and booze." According to him, "This money is too hard-earned to benefit somebody else." When Alberto has sex with men he does not like, he "gets rid of the bad taste" by rewarding himself with a good prize. "If I gave it all to my brothers and sisters, I couldn't put up with this shit," he confesses.

However, there are other reasons. Although Martin assured us that his mother does not suspect how he earns his money, she actually came looking for him at the brothel. She stayed outside, but yelled for him from the street. Martin, scared to death, asked the doorman to tell her that he had already left.

The truth is, Martin's mother knows what her son is up to. The same thing happened with Mono's girlfriend, who showed up while he was with a client. Despite the fact that some family members and lovers know the probable origin of the young men's incomes, one reason that Martin and others like him are secretive about this money is that they do not want to share it. Their household needs are so great that the budget does not allow for "luxuries," as Martin calls them. Instead of feeling guilty about going to the movies with their girlfriends, or buying a pair of nice jeans, the guys prefer to conceal their earnings and pretend that they received gifts or were treated by friends.

Cerebrón represents the other extreme. He averages ten clients daily, including those from the sauna where he works during the day, and those from the brothel at night. His price is higher than Martin's. Cerebrón charges 5,000 colones for masturbation or oral sex, and 10,000 colones for active anal sex. What is the difference? He explained:

> I'll be honest. Not everyone can charge the same because not everyone has this [he grabs his crotch]. Clients choose me because I'm good-looking and because I can give them a good twelve inches of pleasure. They're willing to pay more for a good hunk of meat. Just like anything else, right? If you go out to eat, you're not going to pay the same for a hot dog as you would for a filet mignon. So, for clients who like a good banging, here's where they can get it.

Cerebrón can make around 30,000 colones a day, after paying the owners of the sauna and Lila. His monthly income is more than half a million colones. He says he spends the money as follows:

- Food: 25,000
- Rent: 40,000
- Clothing: 10,000

- Transportation: 10,000
- Contribution to his mother's household: 40,000
- Cigarettes and liquor: 20,000
- Drugs (crack):   50,000
- Miscellaneous (including video games
  and pool):   30,000
- Girlfriend: 50,000
- Savings: 100,000

| Total | 375,000 |

Although Cerebrón claims that this is his budget, there is a discrepancy of 125,000 colones between what he assures us he earns, and what he says he spends. One explanation could be that he does not earn as much as he claims. Another explanation could be that he "launders" part of his income. The laundering might be done by purchasing luxury items for himself. He wears a gold chain, nice clothes, and even has a beeper so he can be located by his clients. In addition, he drinks a fair amount and does more crack than he would like to admit. According to Lila's reckoning, Cerebrón spends up to 5,000 colones a day on crack and another 3,000 on video games and pool bets.

Cerebrón's girlfriend knows what he does for a living. However, she does not suspect how much money he makes. If she knew, confesses Cerebrón, "I'd have to spend more on her and help her with her household expenses." He therefore prefers not to declare everything he makes so that he can spend it on himself:

> Give me a break! I'm not going to spend all day sucking dick to have to share the money. Nobody knows how difficult this job is. Everybody thinks you go around laughing your head off and not doing anything.

Cerebrón has occasionally managed to put 100,000 colones into his savings account. He is the only *cachero* with a bank account. If he were able to control his crack habit, he could buy a house in the future. This is his dream: "I'm sick of living in a dump—I want to put the things I've bought [a television, a bed, a stereo system, dishes, and clothes] in a place of my own."

Ernesto is an "in-between" case. He charges 2,000 colones per client and specializes in oral sex and masturbation. His monthly income is therefore much lower than Cerebrón's (around 80,000 colones). Hardly any of this money is left at the end of the month: "It all goes on food at home, alcohol, and drugs." His family believes that he is unemployed and that he earns an irregular income by doing odd jobs. He is barely able to contribute 10,000 colones a month to the family budget.

According to Lila, Ernesto smokes up to 5,000 colones' worth of crack every day. His income is not always sufficient to support his habit. He is often seen selling items from the house or stolen goods. Sometimes his crack consumption goes down and he can buy some of the things that he needs. However, this does not usually last long.

There are differences in the *cacheros'* incomes. Some, like Cerebrón, can, in theory, save up enough to buy their own houses. Others, like Martin, spend everything they earn on food and necessities. The majority, like Ernesto, could aspire to a lower-middle-class lifestyle. However, their drug dependency often undermines these aspirations. For others, such as Luis, for whom addiction is not an issue, prostitution allows him to pay the tuition for his accounting degree.

When *cacheros* are not involved in drugs, they usually spend their money on other items. Mono, for example, spends more money on pool bets than on drugs. The game has turned into a vice that he cannot give up. He is often seen pawning his girlfriend's clothing to pay his debts. Others spend excessive amounts of money on video games. Daniel is addicted to them and spends up to 50 percent of his earnings on video games.

When we asked some of the interviewees what they would do with the 5,000 colones from each interview session, they told us that they would save it and that this kind of money "isn't spent so quickly." When we asked why this money lasts longer, they explained that it was because it was "legitimate," as it did not come from prostitution. Then we asked them: "How would you rather earn 5,000 colones: in a fifteen-minute masturbation session, or an hour with us?" The response was unanimous: they preferred to spend an hour in an interview than to go with a client.

There is a moral component to money management. Many *cacheros* feel guilty about practicing prostitution and regard the money they earn from it as ill-gotten or inferior to money earned in other ways. This explains, in part, their compulsion to get rid of it and their inability to use it for their own good. Money becomes a symbol that must disappear as soon as it appears. The almost unanimous view was that money from prostitution was "dirty" and that prostitution is "a sin." The *cacheros* usually mention the Bible as their reason for feeling that way, and most consider themselves religious. Some go to Mass and to confession. Others do not, but they consider themselves Catholic or Christian.

Although prostitution is a lucrative business, the above-mentioned factors tend to undermine the sound investment of earnings. But perhaps the most important factor of all is age. *Cacherismo* is a profession of extreme youth. *Cacheros* are at their peak between the ages of twelve and nineteen. Beyond this age, their incomes start to decrease. Clients prefer "hairless" boys in the Greek style. When the first signs of age begin to appear, the *cachero* loses his appeal. The young men find themselves with lower incomes precisely at the time when they begin to marry, settle down, or mature. The very factors that would encourage them to "settle down," as Mono says, are those that threaten to destroy them. At the point when they are having children or setting up a home and need more money, *cacheros* are losing their appeal. In addition, their addictions become harder to control. For many, the combination is often lethal.

Chapter 2

Cacheros Are Masculine

Cacherismo is a sexual discourse. By "sexual discourse" we mean all the ideas, principles, notions, myths, and symbolism different cultures formulate about sexuality in different spaces and at different times. Sexual discourses are present in every culture and are one of the main factors that shape it. This means that the specific sexual behavior of an individual in a given culture is partly the result of his own assimilation of these discourses.[1]

In the sexual culture of this brothel, homosexual practices do not threaten the young men's "heterosexuality." Among lower-class adolescents who work in prostitution, there are important divisions between active and passive sex, and between masculine and feminine. They do not consider that their practices determine a sexual orientation different from anyone else's.[2]

Cacheros have a split vision of how men and women should be. They believe that men are strong and aggressive, and that women are gentle and passive. However, they are aware that not all men and women fit into these categories. Nevertheless, the gender division between masculinity and femininity is there. To find out how they view men and women, we asked them to draw a typical man and a typical woman, and then a typical homosexual. Next, we asked them to write a list of characteristics of men and women. Then, we asked them to do the same for homosexuals. Finally, we conducted a visualization in which they imagined that they had turned into women and, as such, walked down a central city street. We have used this exercise effectively with other populations to measure their degree of animosity toward the opposite sex. Generally, chauvinistic men encounter serious difficulties even thinking about being turned into women, and usually do not do the exercise.

When we asked Mono to write a list, from 1 to 10, describing a typical man, the first thing that came into his mind was "chauvinistic and arrogant." His list was as follows:

1. Chauvinistic and arrogant
2. Party animal
3. Thinking about soccer
4. Dances to seduce women
5. Always thinks he's right
6. Is nosy, but denies it
7. Is never content with just one woman
8. If he can, he seduces his friends' women
9. Has no defined personality
10. Has little faith in God until he really needs help

When we asked him to do a similar list for a typical woman, he wrote:

1. Concerned about her looks
2. A gossip
3. Unpredictable in her thoughts and actions
4. Jealous, and only she is right
5. "Very religious" [in quotation marks]
6. Men, men, men
7. When she's pregnant, she thinks she's no longer attractive to men
8. A liar
9. Sometimes thinks she's better than other people

Gato sees men as "strong, serious, hard-working, masculine, honest, daring, brave, ugly, and hairy-chested." Women, on the other hand, are defined more by their body than their personality: "long hair, intelligent, very sexy, thin, not very tall, pretty, exotic, green-eyed" (maybe he was thinking more of the ideal woman than the typical woman). Harold also sees men as "chauvinistic, womanizing, quarrelsome," and women as "beautiful, loving, intelligent, cautious, with a lot of hang-ups, reserved, and thoughtful."

Although their views of the sexes are polarized, they are aware of certain contradictions. Mono recognizes, for example, that men can also be "gossipy." He believes that "some women feel that they are superior to men." Harold thinks that women "are very rarely self-sufficient or see themselves that way." Luis accepts that some typical men "cook" and that women "also like to work and study."

The drawings by Gerardo of men and women reflect the same dichotomy. The typical man for *cacheros* is masculine and muscular, while the typical woman is feminine and a sex object. (See Figures 2.1 to 2.4.) When they were asked to visualize themselves in a woman's body, the type of women they turned into were young, feminine, and provocative.

We used the following exercise:

> Close your eyes and breathe calmly. Don't think about anything for a few moments, just pay attention to your breathing. Once you feel relaxed, imagine that you're standing naked in front of the mirror. Now, using the power of your imagination, picture yourself slowly turning into a woman. Look at yourself in the mirror with the body of a woman. Think that you're a woman who is naked before her mirror. What's your name? Look at your hair, face, breasts, genitals, legs, backside . . . Now start choosing the clothing you want to wear. Think about the blouse, skirt, dress, pants, etc. that you're going to put on. Then imagine that you put on makeup and perfume and get fixed up to go out. Think carefully about each one of these steps as you get ready. . . . Once you've finished getting dressed and getting ready, you're going to imagine that you go outside on the street and walk around for a while. You notice that men turn to look at you and say things. Think how you feel, what you do, and how you walk. . . . Now stop for a moment to wait for a man. What do you feel? What is this man like? Now, little by little let's slowly return to reality. When you feel comfortable, you can open your eyes . . .

The following is a literal transcription of Luis's answers to the questions concerning the exercise:

FIGURE 2.1. Hombre Típico (Typical Man)

FIGURE 2.2. Hombre Típico (Typical Man)

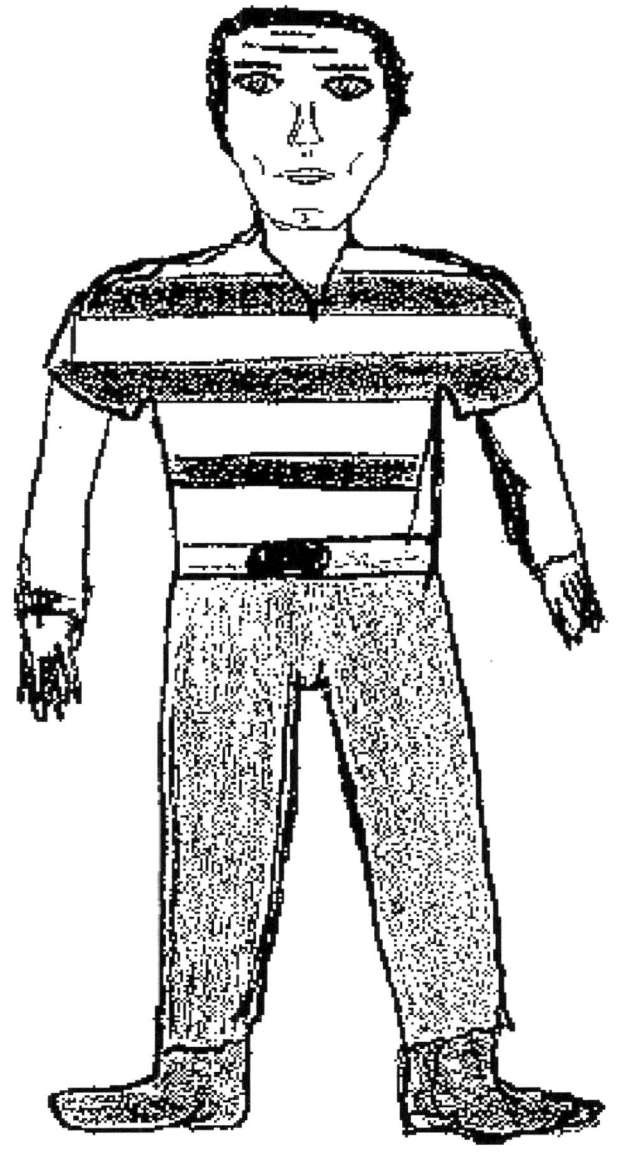

FIGURE 2.3. Mujer Típica (Typical Woman)

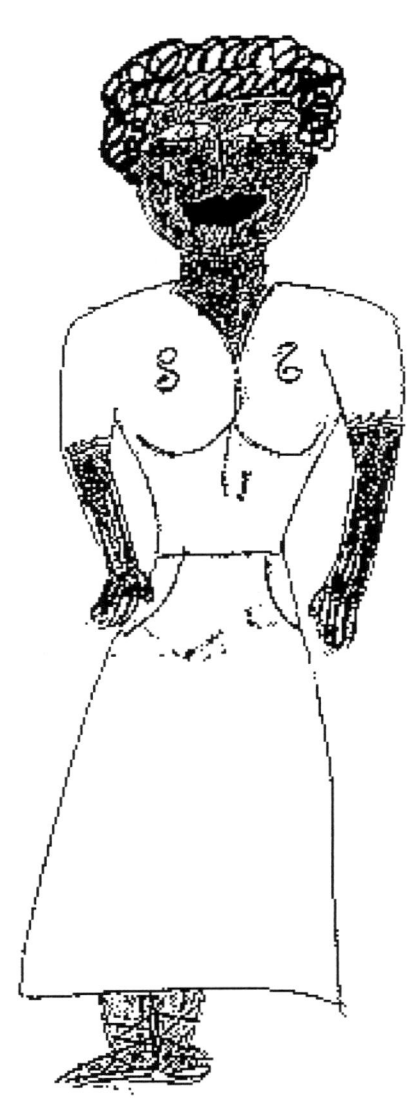

FIGURE 2.4. Mujer Típica (Typical Woman)

2nd Interviewer: Okay, Luis. How did you feel seeing yourself as a woman in the mirror?

Luis: Well, it's a different feeling, a very different feeling, and your heart beats differently. I saw myself in an amazing way, because I saw myself as a woman . . .

2nd Interviewer: Let's talk about clothing. What were your clothes like?

Luis: Well, it was a—what do you call it?—a dress that clings to your body.

2nd Interviewer: Lycra.

Luis: Lycra on the body, but made of fabric, no made of . . . that, but with an open back, it came down to the front of my breasts, er, with half of my breasts inside the other half out. The dress looked good, it was white, red shoes, very provocative.

2nd Interviewer: Were they high-heeled or low?

Luis: High, and the bra was, well, I wasn't wearing one . . .

2nd Interviewer: You weren't wearing a bra . . .

Luis: Because it was like a thread, and I wore a red and black G-string.

2nd Interviewer: So the panty was like a G-string.

Luis: It was a thong.

2nd Interviewer: A thong?

Luis: Yes, but like a G-string, red or black.

2nd Interviewer: Red or black?

Luis: Yeah, the shoes were red.

2nd Interviewer: Okay, let's move on. Sit down in front of the mirror and apply your make-up. How did you do your makeup?

Luis: I hardly put any on, because I looked . . . well, I looked nice with or without makeup.

2nd Interviewer: Did you put a little on?

Luis: Just a little, lipstick and . . . what do they call that, um, blusher, a little . . . and perfume.

2nd Interviewer: You put on perfume?

Luis: Yes.

2nd Interviewer: What was it like, what . . . what was the perfume called, do you know?

Luis: Sweet Honesty, something like that.

2nd Interviewer: Sweet Honesty! [In the United States in the 1970s, this perfume, an Avon product, was marketed to teenagers.]

Luis: Sweet Honesty.

2nd Interviewer: Does this perfume exist?

Luis: Yes, it's for refined women.

Hugo also pictured himself as a very feminine woman:

2nd Interviewer: Hugo, how did you feel when you saw yourself as a woman?

Hugo: Very strange, like it wasn't me, but I was changing into a woman.

2nd Interviewer: What was she like? Try to tell me her age, describe her.

Hugo: She was seventeen, tall, long black hair down to her backside, smooth skin, green eyes, flat nose, round face, big buxom breasts, her vagina was hairy, closed, virgin, and she had a very big backside.

2nd Interviewer: And was this young virgin anything like you?

Hugo: In some ways, in her personality. Sometimes . . . good, but sometimes she changes, becomes pompous, a pain, a person nobody can put up with.

2nd Interviewer: What did she do for a living?

Hugo: She was a pediatrician.

2nd Interviewer: And now tell me, how was she dressed?

Hugo: In a long skirt clinging to her body, a top, and a jacket on top.

2nd Interviewer: What color was the skirt?

Hugo: The skirt was black and the top was white.

2nd Interviewer: Now tell me about her makeup.

Hugo: She had red lips, blue eyelids, a very pretty blush.

2nd Interviewer: Did you like yourself as a woman?

Hugo:	Yes.
2nd Interviewer:	Were you feminine?
Hugo:	Yes, completely feminine.
2nd Interviewer:	Your shoes, what were they like?
Hugo:	Red, with high heels. But a special type, because I had problems with my feet.

In the case of Mario, it was not only easy for him to imagine himself as a sexy, refined woman, but he also learned about the violence experienced by "the weaker sex" and how women feel when men harass them in the street. Although Mario could perfectly well imagine himself as a woman, he thought it would be horrible to become one. His worst fear is to end up as a transvestite. His narrative is so vivid that it is worth transcribing it in its entirety:

2nd Interviewer:	Okay Mario. How did you feel during this visualization, as it's sometimes called?
Mario:	Bad, bad, bad . . .
2nd Interviewer:	Okay, you don't have to say it three times. Why bad?
Mario:	Well, because you really see what it's like to be a woman, a female, the lack of respect that society, that men, show women, the nasty things they say to them.
2nd Interviewer:	Okay, let's take it step by step. First, what is the girl's name? Could you give her a name or not?
Mario:	No, I left it blank.
2nd Interviewer:	How old is she?
Mario:	Twenty.
2nd Interviewer:	Describe her.
Mario:	Fair complexion, a voluptuous, exquisite body, nice ass, luscious shiny lips, with lots of jewelry, earrings, emerald and diamond rings to accentuate her beauty, to make her more playful and provocative.
2nd Interviewer:	What were her breasts like?
Mario:	White with little pink points, delicious.
2nd Interviewer:	Large or small?

Mario:	Medium.
2nd Interviewer:	What was her stomach like?
Mario:	Like a movie star, incredible, her crotch was almost hairless, shaved, with a white G-string.
2nd Interviewer:	Ah, she had a white G-string! And what about her legs?
Mario:	Delicious legs with soft, delicate skin, like a baby, no marks.
2nd Interviewer:	Okay, so that's the woman. Now let's see how she was dressed. But before we do that, I want you to tell me if this woman was you.
Mario:	Well, mentally yes, the mind can do things like that, we completely agree on that point.
2nd Interviewer:	Okay, let's see. The woman you were thinking of, how was she dressed?
Mario:	In a green silk blouse with a low neckline, no bra, a black leather skirt, a white G-string, high-heeled leather boots that come up to her knees, and a brown leather purse.
2nd Interviewer:	Sounds more or less like—this is my opinion—the women in sadistic movies with whips in their hands.
Mario:	Yes, but this woman is more refined.
2nd Interviewer:	Why refined? What does she do for a living?
Mario:	Well, she works in tourism, but she's different when she goes out dancing or on a date or goes out on the street. She tries to look prettier and more provocative, but always in a decent, respectable way, with style, which is what characterizes her, so any man—whether handsome, ugly, rich, or poor—will like her.
2nd Interviewer:	And how is this woman's sex life?
Mario:	Hot!
2nd Interviewer:	Does she go up or down stairs to go out on the street? Where does she live?
Mario:	In a nice apartment, nicely arranged, the way she is, and she goes downstairs to leave her apartment.

2nd Interviewer: What neighborhood is it in?

Mario: Los Yoses, in San Pedro [note: a very exclusive suburb of San José] . . . she hails a taxi and goes down Central Avenue, stopping the traffic. She pauses at several boutiques or shops to look at clothing; she hears the men's catcalls.

2nd Interviewer: Let's stop there for a moment. The woman passed by a group of men. Tell me about these men. What were they like? Where were they? What were they doing?

Mario: Punks from the Soda Palace [a downtown diner] who always hang out on the street corner making rude comments to women.

2nd Interviewer: And what did they say? Tell me exactly.

Mario: Well, they said what a piece of work she was, how much did she charge, that she was out very early, that she shouldn't be out until later at night.

2nd Interviewer: They thought she was a whore?

Mario: Yes, but they didn't realize that she was a sexy, elegant woman and that she didn't dress like that because she was a whore, but because she liked to. Anyone can dress sexy if they want to, but the problem is that they're just a bunch of punks.

2nd Interviewer: Mario, when you did the visualization just now you told me that you felt bad. Why?

Mario: Oh, no, no—for a man to try to be, or to even want to be a woman is awful. At least I personally don't like it.

2nd Interviewer: Why not?

Mario: I don't go along with that, I don't.

2nd Interviewer: But why not?

Mario: Because it doesn't make sense. For me, it's dangerous to feel like a woman, because after maybe twenty visualizations, you realize that you're dressing like a woman. How do you

	think transvestites and all of those types start out?
2nd Interviewer:	So if we do this exercise twenty times you think might become a transvestite?
Mario:	Not exactly, but you start thinking about things and putting ideas into your head, and after talking about it so much and everything . . .
2nd Interviewer:	Okay Mario. Don't worry, because this is the only time we're going to do this kind of simulation.
Mario:	Good!

Among other groups with whom we did this exercise, we found that the masculine men are the ones who have the least difficulty with the idea of a sex change. Those who are not very sure of their masculinity generally do not do the visualization or say that they can't imagine themselves in a woman's body. Therefore, it is not strange that these *cacheros,* who are extremely masculine, did not have any problems imagining themselves as women. However, it is interesting to note the ease with which they did it, and the richness of images they described from the perspective of their new, totally feminine personalities.

When they were asked, after the visualization, if they thought they possessed any of the qualities of the women they imagined, the answers were generally negative. Despite the ease with which they visualized themselves in women's bodies, they did not admit to having any feminine traits.

2nd Interviewer:	Now we're going to ask some questions that are a little more complex. Let's forget about the girl. I want you to tell me which traits of the opposite sex, that is, which feminine traits, you think you possess.
Mario:	Possess, well no . . . No, I don't have any.
2nd Interviewer:	Okay, think carefully . . .
Mario:	No, I just don't have any.
2nd Interviewer:	You don't have anything of the opposite sex? Nothing you do that is similar to the opposite sex, your activities . . . ?

Mario:	No.
2nd Interviewer:	Well, you go to bed with men, don't you?
Mario:	Yeah, but that's different.
2nd Interviewer:	Women don't go to bed with men?
Mario:	Yeah, but they also go to bed with women.
2nd Interviewer:	Maybe that's something you have in common with women.
Mario:	Well, in a way, if you put it like that, then, of course, I have to say yes. But apart from that, nothing. . . .

Because these young men see a world polarized by the masculine and the feminine, everything that goes against masculinity is looked upon badly. Their definition of a homosexual is a man who resembles a woman. Luis's list characterizes the typical homosexual as follows:

1. Has breasts
2. Big backside
3. Hairless legs
4. Very fine features
5. Small hands
6. Long hair
7. Very feminine
8. Refined voice
9. Delicate nose

These views about gender affect the way in which *cacheros* behave and act. Their way of talking, acting, relating to others, and expressing themselves is extremely masculine. Jonás tells us that he even exaggerates sometimes, because he does not like anything feminine. When we asked him to act out a scene of how a "macho" man is picked up by another man, and continues to act masculine, this is what happened:

2nd Interviewer:	Now I want us to talk. We're going to do a role play. I'm the client and you're the prostitute. We're going to talk about money. We're in the park, we've already met and spoken to each other.

	Now we're looking at each other and we start talking . . . Look, how much do you charge?
Jonás:	Depends what you want.
2nd Interviewer:	Hey, I don't know what I want yet. Why don't we just go to the room?
Jonás:	Well, the price is five thousand.
2nd Interviewer:	And what does that include?
Jonás:	Everything except penetration.
2nd Interviewer:	You can make love to me for five thousand?
Jonás:	With a condom.
2nd Interviewer:	Okay, thanks. That's fine—but I have a problem. I don't have the five thousand, but I want to go with you. Can't you give me a discount?
Jonás:	No . . . but, how much do you have?
2nd Interviewer:	Well, I could give you three.
Jonás:	Three thousand . . . Okay, fine—as long as you don't ask for too much when we're in bed, and you don't ask me to do things I don't want to do. I only do things I want to do.
2nd Interviewer:	Thanks, Jonás. [The role play is over]
Jonás:	That's how I have to be: cold and serious.
2nd Interviewer:	You don't smile or anything. Why not?
Jonás:	No, because smiling is like opening a door or giving them an advantage or something like that. You have to be cold, and if you say "no," it means "no."
2nd Interviewer:	If you see someone smile like that, what do you do?
Jonás:	No, for me that's embarrassing.
2nd Interviewer:	To smile?
Jonás:	It's embarrassing because you can smile at whoever you want, but suppose the other person who's smiling at you is a raving queen and everyone is watching him and then you smile at him . . . and if you're a good-looking guy and you look at a girl, what a joke! They're going to think that I'm the same, so it's better

	if I act serious and if they want me fine, and if
	not, fine.
2nd Interviewer:	So if you smile you lose points.
Jonás:	As far as I'm concerned, you lose points.

For Ernesto, it's not smiling that *cacheros* should avoid, but walking like a "queen." He believes that a man should walk proudly, "showing he's got something between his legs. People should know they're looking at a real man." Daniel shares the need to always act masculine. To him, being "macho" is "not letting a man touch your ass or kiss you." Men, according to him, "were not born to be fucked or fondled." To his way of thinking, real *cacheros* penetrate without hesitation. Mono, on the other hand, thinks that masculinity "is inborn." He thinks that there's "nothing you can do to look masculine." "Look at Lila and me. I don't move or talk like a queen. He was born that way."

Two factors become important in projecting the *cachero*'s virility: sports and reproduction. Sex workers' sports are "macho"—pool, soccer, basketball, and boxing. Panameño is a serious soccer player who plays aggressively. "I can't imagine a faggot playing like I do, or training like I do," he says. "Soccer is a masculine sport. You can get pounded in a first-division game, and you usually get more knocks in one night than in all the faggot sports put together." Mono agrees: "You're not going to see any gays playing soccer, or boxing, or even playing pool. Those are aggressive men's games. Nobody puts up with effeminate guys." One of the characteristics that Jorge strongly associates with masculinity is playing pool. Pool halls are among the most sexist places in Costa Rica. It is very unusual to see a woman playing, or even watching the game. Pool halls are exclusively for men, particularly for the most "macho" men, according to Mono. "It's not that it's a particularly aggressive sport or that it requires a lot of physical strength," he continues, "but it's played in a macho environment. No faggot would even try to come in here; chicks either. The players don't like them."

Through reproduction, *cacheros* proclaim that they are different from their clients. Although they are aware that some of their clients are married and have children, gays for them "don't have families."

Cacheros, on the other hand, have them "early on." This means that they become fathers at a very young age—most of the interviewees over fifteen already had children. Some claim that they do it because they want to. "You have a natural desire to give a kid to the woman you love. It's a natural part of life," says Pedro. Others, like Daniel, think that "People respect you more as a man when they see you with children." According to Mono, "the chick's belly is a sign that you fucked her and got her pregnant."

Cacheros regard homosexuals as similar to women, and describe their physical attributes more than their mental or professional ones. Unlike *cacheros,* homosexuals are feminine. Panameño considers them "vain," "jealous," "loving," "concerned with details," and "stupid." Mono is less inclined to stereotype homosexuals, but he also believes they are "more human," and that "they tend to get along better with women."

When asked to draw a homosexual, they portrayed a very effeminate man or a transvestite. (See Figures 2.5 and 2.6.) To them, homosexuals are men who reflect characteristics of the opposite sex and who feel desire for other men. The prostitutes see themselves as *cacheros,* "bisexual," or "male." In other words, they do not mix gender characteristics and they court women in public. Noé does not consider himself homosexual because "I'm not attracted to men." Erick defines himself as "100 percent pro-vagina." Luis thinks he is heterosexual because he feels attracted only to women. Mario considers himself bisexual, but his definition is based on the fact that he enjoys penetrating both men and women. For him "having sex with a woman or with a man is the same . . . the ass is what I like."

For Tío, being gay means "feeling like a woman." According to him, there are various degrees of "gayness." The most extreme case is a "queen" who is obsessed with being a woman. Tío is well aware that there are many types of homosexuals and that being gay is not synonymous with being effeminate. However, what makes him different from them is that "I don't like other men and I don't turn to look at them on the street, like they do." Tomás agrees that it is the harassment of other men and the rejection of women that determines homosexuality and that prevents him from being homosexual.

These different perceptions of homosexuality amount to more than a simple appraisal. They reveal the cultural basis of a discourse on

FIGURE 2.5. Homosexual Típico (Typical Homosexual)

FIGURE 2.6. Homosexual Típico (Typical Homosexual)

gender and sexuality. People are divided, not in terms of personality or sexual practice, but in terms of their physical power. Men are those who control other men and women. For this reason, *cacherismo,* as an aspect of this model, does not generate any contradictions. A *cachero* is a masculine male who exercises sexual power over another man. However, for them and those around them to accept them as *cacheros,* there must be a hierarchy of power in which the prostitute symbolically imposes his rules. For sex workers, homosexual practice does not make them gay, or homosexual, or even bisexual (although they use these words, the meanings they assign to them are different from those widely understood[3]). As long as sexual desire is expressed for the opposite sex and their behavior is masculine, they continue to be male. Those who express desire for other men or are effeminate are "queers," "gays," or "homosexuals."

Lila's brothel is located in a marginal area of San José, where there are few job opportunities. Most adult men are unemployed for much of the time. Thus, young people and adults from marginal communities, who have few possibilities of studying, making money or acquiring social prestige, exercise their power through the one and only thing they possess: their bodies. But this must be done in a masculine way, and therefore they need to differentiate themselves from homosexuals and women.

In this regard, the prostitutes are tacitly tolerated by their community. In marginal areas, gender definition is based more on physical force and the body than on psychological factors. In other words, a man is a masculine being and a woman is a feminine one. A feminine man is equivalent to a woman, and a masculine woman to a man. Gender is polarized by the use of force and physical control (of women), and less by specialization and supposedly distinct psychologies. This explains why essentialist views on gender are more acceptable among the lower classes than among the middle classes in Latin American societies: people are born that way, and they stay that way. The Freudian concept of gender and sexual orientation being learned does not exist.[4]

In this way, prostitutes are tolerated in the community. They are masculine, play manly sports such as pool and soccer, get married, and have children. *Cacheros* do not openly question gender models. It is interesting to observe that the other clients of nearby pool halls, who know that the *cacheros* work at the brothel, do not discriminate against them or reject them as fellow players. This is not the case with Lila, who is regarded as a "queen" for being exclusively homosexual and effeminate. Ernesto tells us that whenever his pool buddies see Lila, they say, "Here comes the stinky queen." Lila, aware of this rejection, has hardly left his house for seven years and never exchanges a word with his neighbors. *Cacheros,* on the other hand, usually wait for their clients in the pool hall next door to the brothel. As the "macho" men play their games of pool, Lila signals from outside that a client has arrived and he needs a masseur. The players pretend Lila does not exist, although they know that a young man will soon answer his call.

Chapter 3

The Rules of *Cacherismo*

The discourse that we refer to as *cacherismo* includes a series of requirements that mark the difference between homosexuality and heterosexuality. These requirements are defined in different ways by the local community, by the brothel owner, by co-workers, by the young men's lovers, by their families, and even by the police who "look the other way." According to this discourse, *cacherismo* is an easy way of making money by having sex with homosexuals.

To ensure that *cacheros* are not seen as homosexual or bisexual, there are certain discourse practices aimed at distinguishing them from their clients. This is done by creating divisions in behavior, practices, and lifestyles. These polarities are not neutral: one has more value than the other. The *cachero*, in theory, stays in a straight social environment, is only temporarily a prostitute, and is masculine, heterosexual, one who controls and exploits clients. The clients are associated with passivity, homosexuality, old age, are permanently gay, may be in gay or straight environments, and are the ones who yield to the desires of the *cachero*. According to this discourse, a *cachero* is worth more than a homosexual.

MATERIALISM

Cacheros have sex for money. José tells us that "Money is all I'm interested in," which seems to be the general feeling. *Cacheros* are not interested in having emotional relationships with men, because "That's what women are for," says Arnoldo. None of them would have sex with men if it were not "for the money," says Mono. None of them admits to having felt any attraction for a man, even when very young. All began their sex lives with women and are sexually and emotionally involved with women, rather than men. Clients, on the other hand, "want you to tell them they're attractive and interesting and I just don't give a shit," confesses Alberto. Miguel cannot conceive of how two men can love each other: "I don't know what they can share if they're the same—it's not logical."

Lila confirms that the workers at the house are naturally heterosexual, but that desire for money and material things has made them bisexual.

1st interviewer:	Tell me something—I've heard you use the word "homosexual" a lot. What do you consider these guys sexually? How would you define them?
Lila:	I'd say they're bisexual, both ways.
1st interviewer:	Bisexual? And how do they see themselves?
Lila:	Militant bisexuals. They don't care about homosexuality—they say they aren't, but they have sex with men, so . . . what are they?
1st interviewer:	But they say they're not.
Lila:	They say they're not because they have women, but they're willing to go with men for money.
1st interviewer:	Are they looking for money or for something more than money?
Lila:	Well, if a very rich guy came along, they would be willing to give themselves up in exchange for living very well, which happens sometimes.
1st interviewer:	But are they looking for something more than money in their relationships with men?
Lila:	Well, a good life.
1st interviewer:	Stability?
Lila:	Stability, which means money.

Andrés, a gay sex worker, does not regard his co-workers as homosexuals, and tells us that most of them are in it for the money.

2nd interviewer:	Deep down, do you consider your co-workers to be homosexuals?
Andrés:	I think generally they're not, they just think about the money.

Finally, Lila believes that sexual tourism and wealthy foreigners who come looking for Costa Rican boys has lured thousands of young men into prostitution.

1st interviewer:	Do you think that money is the motivating factor here?
Lila:	Absolutely, 100 percent.
1st interviewer:	So, if they had money, they wouldn't be going to bed with men?
Lila:	If they weren't being paid it would be less likely.
1st interviewer:	No, no. If the guys had enough money, they wouldn't go to bed with men?
Lila:	Maybe not, but their ambition to always have more makes them do it. In all these seaside towns that are in the tourist guides, it's very common to find rich homosexuals from Europe or the U.S. who come looking for the rugged "macho man" that you don't find in the city. They also come to escape the fear of AIDS, so they go for peasants instead of the gays you find in the bars of big cities. The homosexual makes the trip and brings the money he's saved to spend on the guys he's going to pick up. And it's all very easy: he invites them out for drinks or to eat, comes prepared with watches, not expensive ones, but he brings cheap watches or gold-plated chains—not real, but gold-plated— and then the guy remarks what a nice chain it is, and he says, "If you like it, it's yours. Here, take it." The guys are fascinated, they end up having a drink with the guy, and they follow him wherever he wants . . .

Masculinity, then, is not an obstacle to all types of men becoming *cacheros*. Where money is involved, anything is possible:

Lila: I'm familiar with the San Carlos area and I'm really amazed when you go through Zarcero or Ciudad Quesada or you get to La Fortuna de San Carlos and any guy accepts a pickup. You see a car go by in Ciudad Quesada, and there can be four to six guys on the corner, the driver goes by and smiles, you know, like an offer. But why's this happening? Because of tourism and foreigners—they're being seduced by tourism. There's a lot of gay tourism all over the world.

1st interviewer: Do a lot of people come?

Lila: A lot—there's no end to it. In 1964, I was working in a house, a rooming house, and once a group of twenty-two or twenty-four boxers came from Golfito, about twenty-four people in all, and the most brazen one asked me if I knew a homosexual—but he used a more vulgar word, a faggot—that a rich guy could spend the night with. So I told him I knew several. I asked him, "You want me to bring you one?" "No," he said. "I want twenty. We're twenty gay boxers." I was stunned. I couldn't believe that in this group of twenty-two boxers from Golfito, twenty of them, all macho, were gay. So I asked him, "How come there's so much homosexuality in Golfito?" He answered, "Ah, it's because of the banana company bosses. They pay guys very well for sex, so half of the people in town are into it."

1st interviewer: For money?

Lila: For money.

When asked to describe a typical homosexual, one of the responses was, as Luis said, someone who "looks for company and pays." Jorge also associates homosexuality with payment of money. For him, the typical homosexual is a man who "throws away his money and doesn't care." Pedro writes them off as "fools," easily deceived by others.

Homosexuals, thus, are those who pay, while *cacheros* are those who charge. "I never do this if it's not for money. The ones who do it for pleasure are the gays," says Mario.

LACK OF CONTACT
WITH THE GAY COMMUNITY

Cacheros are not part of Costa Rica's gay community. They stay away from gay bars, clubs, activities, organizations, or hang-outs. José, for example, emphatically denies having set foot in a gay bar. Mono has been only once in his whole life, and says he does not like gay bars:

> I'll say it again, the type of homosexual and the type of scene I like is very limited . . . I'm not prepared to go to certain bars or clubs where there are a bunch of homosexuals who, after two, three, or four drinks are already falling apart and who think they can come and grab and squeeze you, and I don't like that.

Mario feels much the same about the main gay bars in San José:

> Well, I tell you, that shithead bar owner is becoming a multi-millionaire. Besides, it's a very dangerous place—dangerous in terms of disease, especially AIDS. And I tell you, these people show up all nicely dressed and talking fancy, they have a few drinks, they pick up anyone who walks by, they grab anybody. Not that I have a lot of experience, 'cause I've only been once, but I've heard comments, and besides I know all those places are dangerous because people get drunk, they grope each other and snort drugs in the bathroom. For them it's a fun place just like a straight club would be for anybody else, you can see that anywhere . . .

Jonás does not go to gay dance clubs because he is afraid of turning into a homosexual:

> I have gay friends I do business with. But they've told me that they started out like I did, for money, and later they began doing it for pleasure. What they did was go to clubs and hang out with gay friends . . . they began to change, they ended up liking it and staying. I try to avoid getting stuck in homosexuality.

Luis does not like to "greet, recognize, or meet clients outside of the brothel." If he walks by a client on the street and recognizes him, he "tries to ignore him." Vernol explains that "I never say hi to a gay on the street." Miguel thinks it's better not to be seen at any homosexual places because "gays start gossiping in front of everybody." Leo confesses that when he sees a client, "I cross the street and act like I've never seen him before." For them, socializing outside the brothel means becoming homosexual. "My mother knows I work in this whorehouse, but she doesn't want me to go to gay parties because then I'll end up like them," says Rodrigo. Some *cacheros* make visits to apartments or private houses. Once the client gives them his phone number, they can make dates. But it is always understood as a visit to a private place for prostitution.

A DAY IN THE LIFE

Since *cacheros* shun gay hangouts, they must look for other "neutral" places where they can pick up clients when they are not at Lila's house. One of the favorite spots is a city park where thousands of people wander by. It is not considered a gay park, although certain sections are known as gay pick-up points. Other spots are pool halls, "mixed" bars, urinals, movie theaters, and certain streets. However, *cacheros* do not have any contact with gay venues such as bars or clubs. There are some like Carlos who tend to frequent houses of prostitution:

2nd interviewer: I want you to think back to the past, to the very recent past and recall what you did on a typical day. Maybe not right now, because you're in the process of moving out, but before when you lived here.

Carlos: Well, when I lived here, I used to get up around two or three in the afternoon, take a bath, drink some coffee and stuff, and if there was nobody here—a client, that is—I would head out for the street.

2nd interviewer: Slow down, we're going too fast here. You would get up at two in the afternoon —so what time did you go to bed?

Carlos: Around three or four in the morning.

2nd interviewer: You got up at two, and let's imagine that there were clients.

Carlos: I'd stay there working and then after I'd go and see what was going on outside.

2nd interviewer: You went out onto the street, and what did you do on the street?

Carlos: I'd walk around, go to a video arcade, where I knew someone would show up.

2nd interviewer: A client, you mean.

Carlos: Yeah. Because sometimes I didn't have enough money on me to do what I was going to do.

2nd interviewer: And what were you going to do?

Carlos: I was going to have a beer, buy drugs, and all that stuff.

2nd interviewer: After that, where did you go?

Carlos: To the brothel.

2nd interviewer: And what was happening there?

Carlos: There were guys watching porno movies, snorting drugs, and drinking. That was the most typical, because that's what we did every day.

2nd interviewer: What time did you leave the house?

Carlos: No, sometimes we stayed overnight there.

Pana, a soccer player who only works at Lila's house, is a very different case. Pana is a family man and an athlete who is a real homebody.

2nd interviewer:	Now we're going to talk about this place. How many hours of your time do you spend here?
Pana:	Eight hours.
2nd interviewer:	And from here do you go anywhere else to do the same kind of work?
Pana:	No, from here I go home.
2nd interviewer:	So you don't go to bars or clubs?
Pana:	No, I don't even drink—well, I can drink two, three, or four beers at the most.
2nd interviewer:	Where?
Pana:	Here, though I'm not a drinker.
2nd interviewer:	Okay, well, what are your favorite fun places?
Pana:	The soccer field, the Parque de la Paz [a park] and the Casa Juvenil.
2nd interviewer:	Pana, if you play soccer for a national team, how do you divide your time?
Pana:	The practice matches before the qualifying rounds are in the morning, until noon, and here we start at two in the afternoon, so I told the owner that if there was a game on Tuesday nights I wouldn't come to work.
2nd interviewer:	So let's divide up the day. What time do you get up, and then what do you do?
Pana:	I go jogging at six in the morning and get back at 7:15. I take a shower at eight, have breakfast, and I stay in bed until noon, doing whatever at home.
2nd interviewer:	And what time do you train?
Pana:	When I have a game, I leave the house at six or seven in the morning, I get to the stadium at eight, we exercise and then we kick a ball around until eleven-thirty.
2nd interviewer:	Do you work here on weekends?

Pana:	Yeah, from two to ten at night, but with a Sunday off in between.
2nd interviewer:	And do you stay here later than ten o'clock?
Pana:	No, I try not to stay later than ten.
2nd interviewer:	Outside of here, what kind of people do you like to spend time with?
Pana:	Just my wife, because I've never liked going out in groups; I've never liked it.

A CLEAN SLATE

Cacherismo in this house is a young person's activity and ends early in life. With just one exception, there are no prostitutes over twenty-five in Lila's brothel. These young men are expected to spend only a few years in this job. Thousands of adult men have practiced this profession without arousing the slightest suspicion. Mono feels that "At twenty-five, I'm already considered a veteran." Arnoldo believes that "You only practice this profession for a while. It's a passing thing. You'll never reach old age as a whore." Carlos knows a lot of men who spent some time at the house but then "left this profession completely."

To prove that this is a temporary job, the *cacheros* have girlfriends, become engaged, or already live with women. The majority have more than one child. Only one admitted to not being in a stable relationship with a woman, but said he did have sex with women. Many of these women know about their boyfriends' work, or at least suspect. Noé admits to "having told her [his wife] what I do for work" to prevent her "hearing it from someone else." Rodrigo's mother knows that her son is a *cachero* and laughs about it, but she wants him to marry a woman. Mono's girlfriend waits for him in the pool hall next to the brothel. "She knows that I do this for money and that I'm not being unfaithful." Whether or not the women know, the interviewees make it clear to others that they have female companions. "I grab my girlfriend near the pool hall so my friends will see—then they know that I'm not queer," says Tomás.

Two factors influence the temporary nature of prostitution. One is that Lila's clients are pederasts and want young men (without facial hair). The other has to do with moral perceptions of prostitution. *Cacheros* consider their work a sin. There is no cultural discourse that allows them to look at their activities as a profession. There is a general consensus in the country that prostitution is negative and sinful. Thus, many of these young men feel "dirty" working in an "easy," "corrupt" profession. As Fernando puts it:

2nd interviewer: So, you work in prostitution to provide a good life for your family?

Fernando: For the moment, yes.

2nd interviewer: Why haven't you tried to look for a different job?

Fernando: I'm looking, but it's very hard for me to find a job.

2nd interviewer: Why?

Fernando: Because I don't have my papers.

2nd interviewer: You're illegal?

Fernando: Yes, I'm illegal.

2nd interviewer: Does being illegal have much to do with your job?

Fernando Of course. In this country you even need papers to be a janitor.

2nd interviewer: Tell me something—can you see a time in the future when you'll be able to leave this profession?

Fernando Sure. When I get my documents, I'll find a good job, and won't have to do this— instead I'll have a real job. This work is very dirty.

2nd interviewer: You see it as dirty?

Fernando: Sure.

2nd interviewer: Why?

Fernando: Because, I don't know . . . sex is something very intimate. You should only do it with someone you love or someone you're married to.

Some, like Jonás, do not see it as a crime:

2nd interviewer: Do you think that money can be good or bad?

Jonás: Depends on how you want to use it.

2nd interviewer:	Do you think money can be badly earned?
Jonás:	The money I earn?
2nd interviewer:	No, any kind of money earned. Are there bad jobs and good jobs?
Jonás:	Well, in my case, the money is well earned because I earn it by making people happy; I'm not stealing or anything. Badly earned money would be from selling drugs or doing things you shouldn't.
2nd interviewer:	You think that money earned from prostitution is badly earned money?
Jonás:	No, it's not badly earned.

However, even he does not regard prostitution as a long-term job, nor does he consider it a respectable profession:

2nd interviewer:	Now, why did you choose this job?
Jonás:	Well, I got into it about a year, year and a half ago, something like that—well, a while ago—just because I was lazy and didn't want to work, and this was easy money. That's why I'm doing this, but there's a limit to everything. Now I'm looking for work. I want to settle down, and when I do, I want to get out of this scene.
2nd interviewer:	What do you mean by "settle down"?
Jonás:	Get my thoughts in order, because at the moment I've got like a blindfold and I can't think. I'm doing it all out of necessity, because by working you achieve lots of goals.

Cacherismo accepts prostitution as a necessary social evil, as long as it is temporary. There is a way to "wash away the sin": by having a wife and children. Children help to excuse prostitution because "It's to feed my family," as Erick says. When a person stops for good, on the other hand, he can be redeemed and his past "erased." Most *cacheros* want to leave the profession when they get married. In theory, for a *cachero* not to end up as a "whore," as Luis says, he must retire "on his wedding day." It should come as no surprise then that they have children so young. Not only do they show the world that they are heterosexual, but they cleanse their souls of any sin.

Another factor that contributes to the temporary nature of the profession is the Christian notion of forgiveness. *Cacheros* believe that their sins are forgiven when they stop their work and repent. By "stopping" work, they mean not prostituting themselves anymore and not having sex with men. Ernesto believes that "God forgives your mistakes when you stop making them." He believes that if he were to die at this moment, he would go straight to Hell. But if he left the profession, "God would understand that I had to do it and he would forgive my sins." The other requirement is repenting your actions. When we asked him how a person repents for something, his answer was, "by feeling bad for what you do." "But how do you know if you feel bad about something?" we insisted. "Well, by knowing that you aren't doing things because you want to," he responded. Doing things unwillingly, then, is proof of repentance. This probably means that *cacheros* manifestation of heterosexuality is evidence of their repentance. "Queers, on the other hand, can't repent because they like sodomy," concludes Erick.

INDIFFERENCE

Upon entering Lila's brothel, the guys sit down to chat and casually greet clients. They show no signs of preference toward any client (with a few exceptions to be discussed later). When we asked Tío if he felt attracted to any particular client, his answer was a definitive "no." Erick tells us that it is the client who decides. "I don't choose." Rodrigo agrees, adding that he feels there are clients who promise things and don't deliver, and that bothers him. But as far as having sex with "guys who are old, fat, bald, or ugly—it's all the same to me." Noé likes to perform anal penetration on his clients: "I'll give it to anyone who wants it." Tomás does not mind them performing oral sex on him: "As long as they don't bite me, any oral sex is good." Arnoldo tells us that he doesn't turn down any client: "Money is money."

When we persisted with the question and asked them to choose between a handsome man and an ugly one, these were their responses:

2nd interviewer: Let's say two clients show up: one is a young man of twenty-five or thirty, very good-looking, with a nice body, and the other is an older man of about sixty, fat, ugly, bald, hairy, and you had to choose between them. Who would you choose?

Pana: No, I don't make any distinctions based on race, or looks, or anything. I have to do my job because that's why I'm here, and I have to get known among the clients because that's how you get popular. I have a big, long penis and I'm a good masseur. If I have to penetrate a client, I do, but I don't let them touch me, I don't care if it's Bill Clinton. They are the ones who choose, not me, so it doesn't matter to me what they're like, as long as they're clean. A young client might have a nicer butt, but I'm not concerned about that. The old guys are sometimes less passionate and more affectionate so each one has its advantages.

Carlos thinks that *cacheros* actually discriminate against younger clients, though that has nothing to do with their looks:

2nd interviewer: Let's talk a little about clients. Is there a certain age beyond which you think they should pay more, or less?

Carlos: No, actually I think that the young ones should pay more.

2nd interviewer: Why?

Carlos: Well, because they're the most difficult. They're more demanding and they ask for more.

2nd interviewer: What do you mean by "young"?

Carlos: From twenty to thirty, thirty-five.

2nd interviewer:	You've had people like that?
Carlos:	Sure, but they're never satisfied, they always want more, and it makes you uncomfortable. The older guys are faster.
2nd interviewer:	So you don't charge them more for being old?
Carlos:	No, the same . . . that is, I tell them the price, and if they're happy, fine, and if not, fine.

When they start to feel a preference for a particular client, they repress their feelings. Luis tells us that there are times when "I like one client more than another . . . but I try to avoid that." When asked why, he answered, "I'm afraid I would end up liking him." The same happened to Miguel, who admits that he has never liked men, but with his lifestyle, he is afraid of becoming homosexual, as prostitution is progressive and "You can end up liking it."

Sex workers are, theoretically, only looking for money in their relations with clients. Almost all had their first sexual experience with a woman (usually much older than themselves) and their childhood sexual fantasies were about women. In order to have an erection with a man, most of them admit to closing their eyes and fantasizing that they are with a woman. At the same time, *cacheros* believe that if they did not fantasize, they would not be *cacheros*. According to Eduardo, "If I didn't think about women when I have sex, I'd be a queer." The imagination confirms that "you don't like men," says Luis. The fantasy, in theory, should last for the entire sex act, and at no time should it be interrupted to enjoy sex with the client, a man. To be "men," *cacheros* must think about women when they are with men, and when they are with a woman, they should not think of anyone else.

One of the main indications that *cacheros* like neither their jobs nor men, are their sexual fantasies. In theory, having sex with a man never enters their minds. This is what Hugo says:

> To do it, I have to imagine that the man is a woman and that's it. When I see a client, I become like a robot and I say to myself, "This is a woman." I say it to myself three times and that's it—what's in front of me is a woman. It's a nice feeling being able to do that because when you finish and you leave the room, you feel like you've had a woman, and that makes

the job more interesting. You feel a lot of energy and adrenaline and you get into a different rhythm through sexual fantasies. Let's say I go in with two guys—I do everything, because then I earn double—I go in with them, and I start changing them into women. I fool my mind into thinking there are two women and I'm happy in bed because I look at the two women and their ass is a tight vagina and their breasts are those of a young girl, small and hard . . .

Despite the *cacheros'* indifference toward clients, there is one highly desired characteristic: cleanliness. The young men complain that what they dislike about many clients is that they smell. The boys get used to the house odors after a while and stop noticing them. Then, when clients come in who smell bad, their odors seem that much worse. "As long as they don't stink, it's okay," says Cerebrón. "The worst is to have clients that stink," confirms Luis. Gerardo explains that the worst part of the job is putting up with bad smells:

Sometimes we get clients that seem like they're rotten inside. There's this Venezuelan that comes now and then. It doesn't matter that he's skinny and ugly, and looks like a monkey. What I hate is that he smells like a sewer and to make matters worse, he's really passive. I have to use a little Sanipine [disinfectant] as a lubricant to have sex with him. How can a person who is supposed to be a professional be such a slob? That's the hardest part of this job. It's not true that the poor are the dirty ones. A lot of them are cleaner than the foreigners. There's one they call "Doña Chepa (the Sewer)" and some of the guys hide when he comes. When someone goes with him, the others chant to him later, "Wash yourself with Rinso; wash yourself with Rinso [soap]."

PAGADORES

Most of the interviewees admit that they prefer clients over forty years of age, or *pagadores* (sugar daddies). A *pagador* is a mature man who pays for sexual relations with someone younger and establishes a relationship with him. The *pagador* is like a father figure. He may lavish attention, clothing, education, and generally concern himself with the young man's well-being in exchange for sex and love. The *pagador* is usually a pederast who likes boys and hairless young men. He is usually masculine and is not involved in the gay community. Generally, these men are married or involved with women. The word *pagador*, however, has taken on various meanings. *Cacheros* refer to themselves as *pagadores* (*pagadores* means literally "payers") when they buy a friend some drinks or pay for a game of pool. According to this other meaning, anyone who makes a friendly offer to pay is a *pagador.*

In theory, to be a *cachero* one must have relations with *pagadores*. This means it must be made clear to everyone that the young man is involved with the other man out of self-interest. However, we know that not all clients are *pagadores*. Many young homosexuals or bisexuals prefer the privacy and clandestine sex of a brothel. There are twenty- and thirty-year-old clients who also frequent the brothel. However, many of the prostitutes refuse to have sex with them. Jorge tells us, "I don't like young guys. I couldn't have sex with them." Vernol believes that "The young guys who come here are very effeminate—young queens who are too demanding and want to be treated like women."

This rejection might appear to contradict the previous point, but it actually reaffirms it. The sex workers feel that if they practice sex with young men of their own age, they would be turning homosexual, and their role as the pursued party would be changing. Although young clients pay, as far as other concerns, the fine line between prostitution and homosexuality is erased. For a *cachero*, there must be a hierarchy and an obvious power structure. An older man has less power because he has lost his youth and "he has to pay," says Hugo. Between two young men, this clear distinction does not exist.

When does a person cross the line between youth and old age? When does he become a *pagador?* There is no simple answer to these questions. Mono has relations with Pedro, an older man who typifies the *pagador*: fifty years old, gray hair, father and grandfather, wears a tie. José, another *pagador* who frequents the house, is younger. He is thirty-eight, single, lives with a woman, and is considered relatively attractive. Are they both considered "old"? According to Mono, yes. Old age isn't just physical. People seem older because of what they do, not because of how they look. Someone who is married and has children "is no longer young," says Martín. Thus, Pedro and José are old—they are *pagadores*. One is a grandfather, and the other is a man in his prime. But in the culture of *cacherismo,* the line is crossed "when you get married and have responsibilities." However, Pedro and José began paying when they were very young. Even at sixteen, they were already paying children for sex. They consider themselves *pagadores*.

However, physical appearance does have some impact. It is interesting to note that the older *cacheros* have relations with the "oldest *viejos.*" Mono, who has relations with a fifty-year-old man, is not sought after by younger clients. José is not interested in Mono because "He's already an old *cachero.*" At twenty-five (or twenty-seven?), Mono can only aspire to *pagadores* who are old enough to be grandfathers. Past the age of nineteen, there must be a visible difference for both parties to feel comfortable. According to José, "I wouldn't go with such an old *cachero* because I'd seem like a homosexual." However, Pedro can have a relationship with Mono because there is an age difference of thirty years between them.

How is it, then, that an effeminate thirty-year-old man can be considered young, while a noneffeminate one is regarded as old? *Cacheros* have the idea that an effeminate man will never grow up and become a true *pagador*, or an adult man. Therefore, some do not wish to have sex with them. A queen, as Luis says, is like a woman and wants to be treated like one. It's different with a *pagador* who is a macho man. A queen is unlikely to establish a father-son relationship with the *cachero*. According to Mono, "A queen wants a macho man to dominate her and treat her like a woman." The *cacheros* in this house are too young to want to establish that kind of relationship.

Cacherismo is strongly influenced by the clients' pedophilia. Clients look for boys between the ages of ten and fifteen. They are the ones who define the limits between youth and old age—a much stricter limit than among other sectors of the population. To be a young adult has little meaning in this brothel. Moreover, the pederasts are usually very masculine in appearance. Therefore, all masculine men over twenty who pay for sex are *pagadores*. Queens, on the other hand, are age-less—they can be young or mature. Although in theory a queen could be a *pagador*, many of the guys feel uncomfortable with them. A case in point is La Preciada (Precious), an effeminate man who frequents Lila's house and likes to penetrate very young boys. However, the *cacheros* are ashamed to have relations with him, and some refuse. "My God! La Preciada has a huge dick and likes to use it. It's embarrassing to be with him. It's like having your own mother abuse you," says Luis. With a queen, says Mono, "people aren't sure if you're there for the money or because you're gay. Besides," he continues, "it's not normal for a queen like La Preciada to be active. It's a waste of a penis."

There are also clients who are not pederasts and who seek mature *cacheros*, so veterans like Cerebrón and Mono can also find work in saunas and other places that cater to the nonpedophile homosexual population.

DIFFERENT SEXUAL PRACTICES

There is no general consensus among the interviewees as to which practices are acceptable and which are not in this profession. However, all of them do different things with their clients and they are aware that clients do certain things that they do not. Naturally, the things they "don't do" are considered repulsive.

The *cacheros* consider passive (receptive) anal sex as something that "isn't done" and which differentiates them from their clients. Vernol says that he has "a huge dick and clients can't wait to be penetrated or to give me oral sex. Very few can take it, and sometimes I spend half an hour trying to get it in. But when I'm in, they shed tears of joy. . . . They're very tough to take something of that size. I couldn't do it." Tomás considers himself "a man" because "I don't give my ass to any queers. If they want dick, they can have it all. I think oral sex is disgusting, and I would never let them force me to suck them." Mono feels the same way. "Homosexuals like anal sex, but not me."

Another aspect of sex with clients has to do with cruelty. The sex workers interviewed admit that they love to hit and mistreat clients and to humiliate them in a variety of ways. Vernol likes to spank their buttocks. Brian makes them perform oral sex. He claws their backs and, when they least expect it, he hits them with a short whip. Rodrigo makes them beg to touch him.

Active oral sex is another way of differentiating themselves from the clients. The interviewees rarely admit to doing it. Most say that it is precisely the clients' enjoyment of fellatio that enables them to have erections. Lila himself acknowledges that the quality of the oral sex performed by clients is what hooks heterosexual youths on male prostitution. Some of the boys in the brothel have been receiving oral sex from clients since the age of ten, before moving on to other practices. "Women don't know how to perform oral sex, and the guys go crazy from the blow jobs they get from their clients," says the brothel owner.

There is also a distinct hierarchy in relation to body fluids. The young men will not accept saliva and they find it disgusting to kiss a man. Noé tells us, "It turns my stomach when I have to kiss a client." Miguel says he never kisses clients on the mouth. "I let them kiss my neck or my legs, but never on the mouth." Hugo says the same thing: "I'm not one of those guys who likes to kiss men."

Semen, however, is no problem. Since masturbating clients is common practice, the interviewees do not mind getting it on their hands or wiping their clients off with a rag. Nor do they have any problem ejaculating in their clients' mouths. And they do not object to having saliva on their penises during passive oral sex.

The interviewees claim that they use condoms with their clients. Most say they would never penetrate their clients without one. However, that is not the case with their girlfriends or wives. One of the main differences in sex with their lovers, girlfriends, or wives is that they do not use condoms. "I never use a condom with my wife. She doesn't know what I do on the street, and she would start to worry," says Marco. Mono is in the same situation: "My lover is very passionate and so am I. Sometimes I've just been with three guys and she wants sex. She doesn't like me to use a condom. She says she likes it as it is, without anything."

However, there are other differences in having sex with females. With women, says Miguel, "you are more affectionate and delicate." Noé feels that women only want you to "give it to them in the vagina. They don't like anything kinky." Vernol has had similar experiences. Only once "I was able to screw my girlfriend from behind. She said she wanted to know how the homosexuals do it. But she never let me do it again. . . . She said it wasn't natural." Arnoldo has asked his girlfriend to let him do it, "but she said it wasn't normal."

It is not very common for women to practice oral sex either. Only a few of the interviewees said that their partners fellate them. "Women don't know how to give oral sex," says Miguel. Rodrigo agrees that they "don't have experience." The guys, however, don't have any objections to performing oral sex. Luis says he loves to "go down on women," and "lick pussy." He would never do that with a client. The same thing happens with Vernol, who says, "I use my tongue a lot before I penetrate my girlfriend. When she screams that she wants it . . . that's it." However, once they ejaculate, they do not have oral contact with the female genitals. "They're full of fluids, and smell strange," says Gerardo.

It is not only by their actions that *cacheros* distinguish themselves from their clients, but also by their words—or rather, the lack of them. Prostitutes usually have sex in silence. "I don't like to talk because I lose my concentration," says Augusto. Cesar thinks that if the client starts asking him to say nice things, he loses it. Vernol does not want to hear "a sound out of the client. Especially if he's effeminate, since I already feel like I'm with a woman." Tomás says he likes to talk dirty to women, but not to his clients. Rodrigo admits that he prefers "not to say a word once the price has been fixed." For *cacheros,* words are a way of becoming homosexual, of going beyond a mere business transaction. Language can become a barrier to imagining that they are with a woman or can turn into an emotional bond that is unacceptable to a *cachero.*

DOUBLE STANDARDS

Cacheros not only engage in different practices with their clients, but also with their women. Although they are not monogamous, they expect their women to be. Wives or lovers must be faithful, and if they are not, they must pay the consequences. Most think that their women do not know what they do for a living. However, even if they did know, this would not give them the right to do the same thing. A *cachero* is, above all, a macho man who dominates both men and women:

2nd interviewer:	We're going to talk a bit about girls. You're in a relationship with a girl now. Tell me how you get along with her.
Jonás:	Very well, because I can't live without women.
2nd interviewer:	How long have you been together?
Jonás:	About four years.
2nd interviewer:	How old are you?
Jonás:	I'm nineteen.
2nd interviewer:	So you started when you were fourteen or fifteen?
Jonás:	No, when I was seventeen.
2nd interviewer:	So it hasn't been four years, but . . .
Jonás:	I mean "going steady," which to me means kissing her and taking her home, and a serious relationship is something else.
2nd interviewer:	Is this a serious relationship?
Jonás:	Well, more or less, but God help me if she finds out what I do, because we're planning to get married and I've had a child with her, so part of the money I earn here also goes to help her out. It's not much, but every little bit counts, even though she never asks me for anything.
2nd interviewer:	Jonás—she doesn't know about this?
Jonás:	No way!
2nd interviewer:	Why? What would happen if she found out?
Jonás:	The relationship would be over, it would fall apart.
2nd interviewer:	What do you do when you smell different, of soap that's not yours or something, or if she notices that you're nervous because you just came from being with a client. Do you think she's noticed anything?
Jonás:	No, because whenever I go see her, I wash up first. I take a shower, I brush my teeth, I

	change, I put on the same cologne I always use with her, so there's no way she could know.
2nd interviewer:	Would you accept her having relations with men the same way you do?
Jonás:	No!
2nd interviewer:	Why is it okay for you, but not for her?
Jonás:	Because it would be like sharing something that's mine.
2nd interviewer:	If you found out she was doing that, what would you do?
Jonás:	If I found out she was whoring with guys, I'd still split up with her—no matter how much I love her.

Pana is even harsher about what he would do to his wife if she dared to do what he does:

2nd interviewer:	We're going to talk about women. You're in a relationship with a woman. Tell me a little about this relationship—whatever you want to tell me, without getting too private.
Pana:	Well, in the beginning, just like any couple, we got along well. I was playing but my team didn't qualify. I came to work here, but our relationship has always been good. Outside our home it's perfect, and also at home, in private. For me the most important thing is to satisfy her, as a woman, as a person, as a housewife, but if I go to bed with her and I satisfy myself first, I'm not just thinking of myself, I'm thinking of my ego as a male, not my ego as a person, or a husband. I have to think about her first, so that I can satisfy her, so that she climaxes, as they say, and then I can go on to my own.
2nd interviewer:	She doesn't know about your profession?
Pana:	No.
2nd interviewer:	Do you think she suspects?

Pana:	No, she doesn't suspect for the simple reason that I told her I was working for a security agency.
2nd interviewer:	What about smells—you must go home smelling like soap or lotion.
Pana:	No, it's always the same, because I'm in the habit of taking a bath before I go to bed. All I do is take out my wallet, take off my shoes, and go straight to the bathroom. She's not keeping an eye on me, because she knows I leave the house at one to get to work by two. Then we finish at ten, and I'm back home by ten-thirty.
2nd interviewer:	Do you keep an eye on her?
Pana:	Yes, before I did.
2nd interviewer:	Why not now?
Pana:	Because I realize that she loves me, and she's going to have my child . . . so there's no reason to watch her.
2nd interviewer:	Would you allow her to have a relationship with another man?
Pana:	No way! Not while she's with me.
2nd interviewer:	And if she had a job like this and you weren't aware of it?
Pana:	If I found out, I don't know if I would kill her or leave her.

Chapter 4

The Realities of *Cachero* Life

A number of factors conspire to challenge the rules of the game in the discourse of *cacherismo*. By promoting changes, these factors undermine physical and spatial temporality, sexual practices, sexual definition, and social attitudes toward *cacheros*.

FANTASY AND PLEASURE

The young men are well aware that to be *cacheros* they must feel desire only for women. Vernol says that he has to think about a woman he likes a lot "to be able to get turned on and go with a man." Hugo agrees and says that he imagines he is with a woman and concentrates on that idea, because if not, "It would be a disaster." Miguel cannot get an erection easily unless "I've met and dealt with the client, and I start dreaming about breasts." Harold has to force himself to think that "this anus is a vagina, that this man is a woman. If not, I couldn't do this job."

Although, in theory, *cacheros* should not think that about being with men, but rather imagine themselves with women, the relationship between imagination and reality is not so clear-cut. They think and fantasize in their heterosexual relationships as well as in their homosexual ones. In fact, we all learn sexual "scripts" for our relationships and *cacheros* are no exception. These scripts are little discourses that tell us what to do and how to do it. Even our own fantasies depend upon them, because, in order to have them, we must use people from real life. These scripts contain both dialogue and images, and it is impossible "not to think of anything," as Mono says, when the prostitutes are with women or only think of women when they are with clients.

In practice, *cacheros* do not think only about women when they are with clients. Furthermore, during the first years of prostitution, it would seem that the imagination is absent. They admit to having had periods in their lives when they "only thought about the sensation," as Pablo says. Those who began at a very early age, such as Guido, who started at ten, were not mature enough to use their imaginations. "I didn't know anything about sex when I was ten, and when they sucked me off, I didn't know what to think. . . . It wasn't 'til I reached puberty, like around fourteen, that I started thinking about women." Others like Carlos admit they have never needed fantasies to enjoy sex: "Why should I think about something else if I like what I'm doing and it feels good?" he says.

Many confess that, for certain sexual practices, they do not need to fantasize. In the case of oral sex, they enjoy it without having to think about whether it is a woman or a man doing it. "Why would I want to imagine anything if I'm getting a blow job?" asks Mono. Luis says the same thing: "It's easier not to think about anything when they're sucking you. During penetration is when you really need to fantasize." Cerebrón shares this feeling and says it's "not necessary to fantasize when you're getting oral sex, whether it's from a man, woman, queer, or the neighborhood calf." Lila explains that the pleasure the guys get from oral sex makes them end up doing everything:

Lila:	That's where Latin women can't keep up, because for a woman to perform oral sex, she has to be real hot, or a maniac, just being an erotic sex maniac she could be very good at oral sex, but a homosexual displaces her, and then when the man isn't gay, the homosexual gives lots of oral sex to seduce him . . .
1st interviewer:	Do you think the pleasure they get from oral sex is one of the things these people are looking for?
Lila:	Yeah, they enjoy it because it's something they don't get from women. A man isn't going to say to a woman "come here and give me a blow job" or "come here and suck me." It's

hard for these macho men to ask, and if they
ask, they don't know if these women are hot
and want to do it. Only a real hot woman can
do it, only a hot woman who's not a "lady" or
who's been with a lot of men learns to suck
like she should. But there's a factor related to
all these things I've told you. It's really an
incredible phenomenon, incredible that nobody knows about it: that these men who are in
it for the money, do it and enjoy it, even
though they never actually admit that they like
it. . . . Maybe they're thinking about women,
maybe they don't take their minds off them,
but it so happens that they let the gay do what
he wants with them. Often these super-macho
types, instead of attacking the homosexuals
and doing the homosexuals like a man, enjoy
the oral sex, and then allow themselves to be
the ones who are abused. It's incredible how
these macho men take it from behind, but they
do, and then they go to be with a woman, they
act all macho with them, and instead of acting
that way with the homosexuals, they let themselves be penetrated.

In the case of passive anal penetration, *cacheros* who admit to
doing it say that they do not fantasize at that point either. "The few
times I've done it, what I do is disconnect, let my mind go blank so it
goes by quickly," says Carlos. Others like Guido have had experiences that make them do without imagination: "I went with a guy
who was handsome and had a nice body. He asked me what I thought
about when I was with him, and I told him that I thought about
women, and he told me it wasn't worth it, and said I should think
about what was happening between us, and I was able to do it."

Finally, fantasies are not always ongoing. As we have seen, during oral sex imagination is not as necessary, and sometimes it is not
necessary at all. During active anal penetration, there are moments
when "you just think of how good it feels to be coming, and not

about who you're with," confesses Mono. At certain points during the sexual act, *cacheros* enjoy the moment without having to think about women. Cerebrón is convinced that active anal sex is better with men, even though he does not like men. "You come faster in a tight ass. When their asshole tightens, you don't care if it's your own grandmother's."

In practice, it is impossible to "only think about women." There are times when the imagination pauses and you are aware of your sexual partner. In many cases, it is not even necessary. According to Luis, it is a lie to say that "you always think about women when you're with men. Since women don't give blow jobs, you can't imagine a woman when a man is doing it," he adds.

However, this does not mean that imagination does not play an important role in prostitution. It is important in the sense that it provides the *cacheros* with scripts to do their job. The fact of having sex with people they do not know or, in some cases, do not even like, means the imagination becomes the instrument that allows them to "function," as Mono says. "The only thing that matters to the client is that you have an erection, not what you're thinking about," he confesses. In order to function, he and most *cacheros* turn to pornography. This is where they find the images that they use most in their erotic dreams.

Since pornography plays a role in educating *cacheros*, this medium is where they learn their sexual discourse. Instead of seeing *cacheros* as divided between imagination and reality, we could see them as practicing a pornographic discourse, with a mechanical sense of sexuality. Both pornography and prostitution emphasize the body and its mechanical functioning. As Mono says, the important thing is "doing it," not what you think about. Pornography is similar: actors and actresses portray sexual fantasies, but they do it in a believable and mechanically "real" way. In men, this "reality" is expressed in their erection and ejaculation, while in women the equivalent expression of pleasure is not so visible or obvious.

The fact that *cacheros* identify with porno actors makes them turn to pornography to have an erection. This identification, in turn, makes the *cachero's* sexuality more impersonal and mechanical. They themselves admit that they have become "sicker and more sadistic," as Luis confesses. Their pleasures have turned "more violent" both with men and women. Mono has taught his lover to do "everything I've learned through pornography. Before she wouldn't kiss my anus, but now she does it and she loves it." Harold brags that he has done many things with his girlfriends that he never even dreamed of. José admits that over time, "my fantasies have changed. They are becoming more and more sadistic and with more women. Before I only thought about one woman. Now I need more to get a good hard-on." Mono realizes that different practices are entering into his sexual fantasies. "I imagine them licking me from behind, biting my ass, screaming, things that I never did or thought about before." Ernesto admits that now "I'm more sadistic in sex."

Pornography also influences the participants in these fantasies. Some *cacheros'* realize that, although they prefer women, "Clients enter into the fantasies once in a while." Guido imagines that he is "with two women and a man. The man is effeminate and I screw the woman in front and do him in the ass." Mono sometimes thinks about an American that he liked "licking me from behind while I do it to my girlfriend."

Practice, in turn, affects fantasy, and vice versa. Pedro realizes that, at certain times, "A client is so good that I start to imagine sex with women getting more sadistic." Mono's fantasies, on the other hand, are more related to touch. He reveals that his secret for getting an erection is kissing his own forearm, "where it's soft and reminds me of a woman's breasts." This helps him to give free rein to his imagination.

The impossibility of always imagining women when they are with men, and the influence of pornography, helps *cacheros* learn to enjoy sex with men and change their minds. A case in point is Noé, an attractive bricklayer. He confesses that he started "because a friend invited me to this bordello," and that never before "had the thought of going to bed with a man entered my mind." Although the first time he had homosexual relations he felt "dirty and ashamed," he slowly changed his mind. "I have to be honest with you. There is nothing better than sticking your penis in a rectum. Women, when they get wet, are so wide open that you don't feel anything. An ass is tight, so you feel more." Mono agrees, saying that homosexual sex is better and more satisfying. "Women are like a bottomless pit, but there are guys who are so tight that you come much better." Carlos feels the same way. "I'm not attracted to men, but physically it feels better to penetrate a man than a woman, that's the truth." Luis confesses that "The contractions of the sphincter make you enjoy your orgasm more." Gerardo says the same thing:

1st interviewer: What's the difference between going to bed with a man and going to bed with a woman?

Gerardo: Before it was very different, because I knew that women weren't so willing to have anal sex. You knew that your girlfriend would only give you her pussy to screw around with. But, I've always liked it in the ass. I don't know why, but I've always liked doing it from behind, and I get more pleasure with a man because you know that sex in the ass is better, more satisfying, tighter—especially if the person has a nice ass. You get really horny, you see where you're sticking it, and you open up the rectum and see how you go in and out so good, and the tighter it is, the better it feels. With a woman it feels great too, I wouldn't trade a woman for a man, but I like sex with men—I won't deny it. Now there are cool women who are starting to take it from behind, but not all of them.

Oral sex is also a source of pleasure. The fact that their girlfriends, wives, or lovers do not want to do it means that sex workers enjoy their clients. Some of them get so turned on that when no clients show up, Marco, for example, says, "I jerk off thinking about the blow job this client usually gives me." Some give each other oral sex when no clients show up, because "You start to miss it."

The pleasure that many of them feel provokes an identity crisis. Rodrigo admits that he has come to enjoy sex with certain clients so much that he feels he is becoming homosexual. Carlos is also having a crisis because he does not enjoy sex with his wife as much he used to. He finds sex with men "kinkier." Tomás has stopped having sex with women since "I've been involved in male orgies.

Imagine what it's like to have someone sucking you in front and in the back, and another one nibbling you all over." Miguel thinks that prostitution has brought out in him "the homosexual that all men have inside."

Vernol is an interesting case. His relationships with men get him into situations where the line between heterosexuality and homosexuality becomes blurred. A gay man once invited him to his house for sex, and, to his surprise, had also invited a lesbian and her partner. The "more feminine" lesbian took off her bra and threw herself on the bed with her nipples erect. The client asked him to "do her," while the more masculine one "wanted to do me with a dildo." "I refused to let a dyke dominate me, but I had to go with the prettier one first and later the other one said I could fuck her, too. I went from one to the other while the guy waited for me to come only in him," he said. With this range of possibilities, Vernol admits that "I had a great time . . . it was a sexual frenzy that night. I didn't even know who I was hot for. I hope that doesn't mean I'm going to become gay," he concludes. "These orgies confuse me."

Prostitution then, has an impact on both fantasy and pleasure. *Cacheros* should only think about women, but reality makes their fantasies become more complex, more diverse, and more bisexual. The actors in their imaginations, whether men or women, become more "masculine," and they become more impersonal, distant, and mechanical in their sexual relations. For example, when Mono draws a woman, he puts a thought-bubble over her head that says "Generally thinking about pleasure and sex." Jorge also sees women as eager for sex: "In bed they're the worst." Pedro considers that "being a slut" is a female characteristic.

When the interviewees were asked to imagine themselves turning into women, the issue of prostitution also came up. They were treated like sex objects by other men. As women, the *cacheros* were harassed by men who yelled "obscenities" and "abuse" at them when they walked down the street:

2nd interviewer: Where did you imagine you were walking?
Luis: On Avenida Central, to get a taxi or bus.

2nd interviewer:	Okay, and when you met up with the guys, with the men and the boys, what did they say to you?
Luis:	Obscenities.
2nd interviewer:	Like what?
Luis:	Like, "What nice tits! Do you want me to suck them for you?"

Harold imagined workers yelling at him: "Hey, sexy! How much do you charge? Come over here and spend some time with us." Luis imagined that a guy had touched his backside. "This guy came up behind me while I was walking and he touched my ass in front of his friends."

Cacheros not only experience sexual harassment in their dreams, which are totally linked to sexuality, but their relationships with women also become more violent and impersonal. Many admit that they have begun to fantasize about other women when they are with their girlfriends or female lovers, or that they imagine men joining in their sexual relations with the women, either as participants or observers. The women in their fantasies are not stereotypically feminine by Latin standards. They are more assertive, verbally aggressive, and sexually demanding. They want sex for its own sake and like to experiment in bed. This "invasion" of strong women into their sexual fantasies is another way in which homosexuality influences their lives. *Cacheros* may continue having their main relationships with women, but these women have become "masculinized" in their desires and their perceptions. The idea that "You close your eyes and think about a woman while you're doing a man," as Jorge says, is not completely true. *Cacheros* may close their eyes and think about a woman, but this woman of their imagination is only a woman in terms of her sex organs. Her behavior, language, and attitudes are those of a man. In this subtle way, homosexuality creeps in.

FLIRTING

Cacheros tell us that they do not care which client chooses them, as long as he pays. However, when we sit with them and a client comes in, there is a logical reaction of satisfaction and pleasure when one is chosen over the others. On one occasion, we could see the disappointment on Mono's face when a client preferred Luis to him. One might argue that joy or disappointment has more to do with the possibility or earning money or not. However, the *cachero's* psychological reaction is more complicated.

When they are sitting in a row and someone comes to "evaluate" them and see how attractive they are, it is almost impossible for them not to be affected by these decisions. The more popular ones' self-esteem is increased and they feel "superior" to the less popular ones. Cerebrón is among those whose self-esteem has been boosted by his popularity with clients. "I can't deny that I feel great satisfaction knowing that they choose me more often," he confesses. Luis also admits he "likes them to have a preference for me. Women never let you know how great you are, like men do." Erick says he had never paid much attention to his buttocks and his penis before. "I've learned to check out not only other men's butts, but my own as well. I've also realized that I have a big, thick dick. No woman ever told me that. But the clients go crazy for it."

The most popular *cacheros* are treated better by Lila and other brothel and sauna owners. They are considered little gold mines because of their earnings and therefore merit more consideration and better treatment. According to Lila, some of the "hottest" guys are usually the most arrogant. They demand better conditions and show up for work "when they feel like it."

In their efforts to attract clients, *cacheros* are eager to display their attributes. Cerebrón, for example, wears tight jeans that subtly show off "his package," as he refers to his penis. José sits with his legs open to achieve the same effect. Carlos usually smiles provocatively. Ernesto displays his rounded buttocks when he turns on the radio. Others make an effort to seem nice. Although all this flirting goes on in a "masculine" context, it is still a way of attracting men.

The desire to be chosen puts an end to the *cachero's* supposed indifference. The line between client/money and client/acceptance becomes thinner. Since they are at the mercy of the clients' taste every day, being chosen represents a source of income and is also a statement of their worth. José confesses that sometimes "I don't even want or need the money, but it still affects me when a client doesn't find me attractive." Mario believes his popularity has helped him with women, as "I feel sure that I'm nice-looking and sexy." Ernesto feels that he has lost his shyness and his shame. "Before, I'd turn red if I had to talk to someone older. Now, after so many clients, it's easy for me to have a good conversation with anybody," he admits.

Seduction and flirting become a part of life for *cacheros* in many of their relationships outside the brothel. Mono confesses that when he is out in the street, he likes to look at attractive guys, and he loves it when they look back at him. "I don't know, it's like a habit. It's not that I want to go to bed with them, but that I've learned to pay attention to the things that make a man attractive." This happens to such a degree that Mono also tried to seduce one of the interviewers:

Mono:	You know something—I like your nice firm ass.
1st interviewer:	What do you like it for?
Mono:	If you behave yourself, I can do you a little favor and give you a good roll.
1st interviewer:	But Mono, isn't it true that you don't like men?
Mono:	Well, I don't like them, but you don't stop looking at bodies, and that's what I like.
1st interviewer:	Why don't we continue with the interview, because this isn't getting us anywhere.
Mono:	We're not getting anywhere because you don't want to. If you wanted to, you'd let me eat that delicious thing.
1st interviewer:	You're quite something, Mono. Let's finish the interview and then you can eat all you want, but with clients. Thanks for the invitation, though.
Mono:	You're the one who's missing out on a prostate massage.

MONEY AND DRUGS

One factor that destabilizes the discourses of *cacherismo* is addiction. Another is money. Many *cacheros* admit that they have no idea where their money goes, and that it is like a drug for them. José confesses, "I get turned on just thinking about the 5,000-colon bill I'm going to earn." Luis says he never regards a man with money as ugly. "It's not just personal interest . . . money makes them seem more attractive." Mono admits he has earned hundreds of thousands of colones and has lost them just as easily by gambling—one of his addictions. Arnoldo confesses that he never has enough money to buy the things he likes, and that buying them is "as good, or better than sex. When I buy a shirt that I like, I feel really good." Noé has no idea where all the money he has earned in this business has gone: "It's like water—it runs through my hands without my even realizing it."

The need for money drives them to sexual practices that are theoretically not acceptable in *cacherismo*. Gerardo, for example, confesses that clients offer *cacheros* more money to have sex with each other:

Gerardo:	I took a bath, had breakfast, and came here. Well, before I came here, I stopped by the Plaza de la Cultura to see if I could make a contact or something. But it was dead, so I came here. I got here around eleven or twelve and Lila was still asleep. He was in a bad mood and told me to come back at two in the afternoon. I went back to the Plaza de la Cultura again, and came back here at two. He was having coffee and he said he had someone for me at four in the afternoon, so when the guy showed up we went to the room . . .
2nd interviewer:	Wait a second . . . What was the man like?
Gerardo:	He was around fifty-five, fat, gray hair, very serious and, above all, very discreet. We went to the room, and he just likes to see shows . . .
2nd interviewer:	Who went in with you?
Gerardo:	The guy and Hugo.
2nd interviewer:	You and Hugo?
Gerardo:	We were in the act, and Hugo and I took off our clothes, and the guy got all excited, and he

	told me to insert my finger into Hugo, but of course I didn't do it. What I did was bend my finger so it looked like it was inside. The act ended, he paid so I had money and I left feeling good.
2nd interviewer:	When you say that "it ended," does that mean he came?
Gerardo:	Yes.
2nd interviewer:	Did you two come?
Gerardo:	No, not us.
2nd interviewer:	And did you kiss?
Gerardo:	No.
2nd interviewer:	And did you get it up?
Gerardo:	Hugo did, I didn't.
2nd interviewer:	Did he ask you to touch each other?
Gerardo:	To suck dick and all that . . .
2nd interviewer:	You to suck Hugo, and Hugo to suck you?
Gerardo:	No, Hugo to do me, because I explained that I don't like to suck or put it in my mouth.
2nd interviewer:	And how much did he pay you?
Gerardo:	3,500 colones. 500 more for the show.

Money is also used to buy something else that has the interviewees trapped: cocaine and crack. Of all the interviewees, only one said he had not used these drugs. The vast majority also smoke marijuana and drink a lot of alcohol. Many admit to feeling "prematurely aged" and "skinny" because they do so much crack. In more than one interview, we witnessed the guys doing drugs for hours. Arnoldo admits to having stolen and pawned his mother's clothes to buy crack. Mono confesses that the first thing that entered his mind when he was paid for the interview was to "go smoke it." Noé says the same thing, and admits he has been addicted for years and is unable to stop completely. He says he even took food from his children's mouths "to buy drugs." Edwin prostitutes himself "to support my habit." Hugo believes that he is not completely hooked on crack, even though he knows he cannot quit. Rodrigo thought that "it wouldn't happen to him" but "now I'm hooked." Gerardo describes his addiction and how easily he fell into it:

Gerardo: I tried crack during a terrible drinking spree. I
                        have a nephew who's a drug addict and he'd
                        sell his mother to smoke crack, if his mother
                        would let him. You end up in a deep depres-
                        sion, and you don't care if you bathe or not, if
                        you eat or if you trade your food for crack . . .
                        if you can sell your pants and your underwear,
                        you sell them . . . if you can sell your socks . . .
                        if you steal from your mother . . . I had this
                        problem. You become like a pack rat, you steal
                        everything from your mother, take all her
                        clothing, things that she gives you and you just
                        don't care about anything . . . if your mother is
                        a good person or a bad person, you don't care.
                        Crack is your only God. Then I got married, at
                        twenty, and it all fell apart because I started
                        having problems just after we got married. We
                        split up, and I got into coke in a really big way.
                        I threw away all the money I had on coke, then
                        crack came out and I started smoking so much
                        that I almost lost my job . . .

1st interviewer: Do you think the other guys have drug prob-
                        lems?

Gerardo: I see them, and it makes me sad to see them
                        going down the same road I did. They're like
                        this now, but it gets worse every day, and there
                        will come a moment when they're going to try
                        drugs just like I did, because in gay parties you
                        see all this stuff . . . your own anxiety gets you
                        started. There's another guy here, Mono, who
                        used to criticize me when I smoked crack. He
                        would say, "Man, why don't you quit that shit,
                        don't do it and this and that," and now I see
                        him doing drugs . . .

Guido describes how difficult it is to quit crack, once you are
addicted. At the time of the interview, he had been smoking crack

for forty-eight hours nonstop. We interviewed him when he took a break for dinner:

> Sometimes, let's say, when you're addicted to drugs, umm, there are days and moments when you do them all the time, it's really hard to stop. The more you do, the more you want, so you don't care if it's three or four in the morning, you'll go out on the street to buy two or three more hits and come back again and then stay up for eight hours. . . . In my case, I come here and smoke a basuko (cocaine or crack cigarette with other additives), and it's not 'til eight hours later that I can sleep peacefully, because it affects your nervous system.

Guido knows that crack is bad for him:

> Well, crack is a drug that destroys people. It's the most addic- tive drug there is, and whoever does it gets wasted in a couple of weeks, hooked on it. I used to weigh sixty-nine kilos, now I weigh sixty-two. . . . With the first hit, I get a great high for a few seconds. Your ears get blocked up, what they call "ring- ing." It sounds like "ting, ting, ting," and then your heart races, it starts to beat faster, and it's a great feeling. . . . The first hit is as good as an orgasm; you're completely spaced out and floating on air. After those first five or ten seconds you start to get paranoid.

When we paid Guido for the interview, we asked him what he would do with the money, what the first thing that came to mind was. His response was unequivocal:

> What I should do with the money is pay off a jacket I have in the pawn shop. I pawned it to buy drugs, and yesterday I went to leave two thousand colones in payment. I still owe two thousand, so I'm thinking about going to pay that off. But, I also want to buy more drugs. . . . An addict always thinks about the possibility of buying drugs. When you see money, you automatically think about drugs. You think, "Man, how great a [crack] joint would be!"

However, on another day, when he had not used drugs, Guido denied being addicted to crack:

Well, there's a big difference because, well . . . let's say maybe I have a broader view of the scene, of drugs, because you have to be in control, and not let the drugs control you so you end up screwed, all dirty, and catching AIDS . . . but especially being dirty. Look, you can be a drug addict, an alcoholic, a pill popper, or whatever, but cleanliness is very important and it's something very personal, and just because you're a drug addict doesn't mean you can let yourself go . . . I feed myself, I eat, I . . . , well right now I don't exercise or anything because I don't have a racket, but . . .

Despite his optimism, when we asked him why he had pawned his tennis racket, he said it was to buy drugs.

Others, like Bryan, are hooked on alcohol and pills:

Bryan: I drank to poison myself, that is, to get intoxicated. They've had to revive me twice.

2nd interviewer: Will you tell me about that?

Bryan: Yeah, see, I'd been drinking and drinking and drinking, and when I woke up I was in the hospital, with tubes and everything, and a stomach pump.

2nd interviewer: Without pills?

Bryan: Without pi . . . well, actually, yes, with pills too. Lots of pills, I took a lot of Roche [the company that manufactures Valium], a lot of Roche.

2nd interviewer: Tell me about that.

Bryan: There was a time when I didn't want to know anything about anyone, not even my family. I was very depressed, about everything, about my whole life . . . I was very depressed and I got a prescription for these Roche pills. A doctor friend of mine got them for me, so I started taking Roche, right? And every day, every day I'd take two Roche. I was like a zombie 'til I became completely intoxicated on Roche pills and ended up in the hospital. I was in treatment for, like, nine months. I was in rehab . . . I didn't go to the psychiatric unit 'cause I'm not crazy or anything . . .

Those who do not abuse crack or alcohol often have a problem with gambling. Video games and betting create many of the same problems as drugs:

2nd interviewer:	Do you spend money on drugs?
Jonás:	Not on drugs, no.
2nd interviewer:	"Drugs" can also mean guaro [a cheap local liquor], visiting prostitutes, video games . . .
Jonás:	Yeah, I play a lot of cards and pool and all that.
2nd interviewer:	Of the 50,000 colones a month you earn through prostitution, how much would you say you spend on cards?
Jonás:	Most of it. Most of the 12,000 colones I make per week, almost half. I have 9,000 left at the end of the month, and I spend almost 5,000 a week on cards.

2nd interviewer:	On cards?
Jonás:	Uh-huh.
2nd interviewer:	And you don't win any money?
Jonás:	Sometimes you win, sometimes you lose.
2nd interviewer:	Do you consider it a vice?
Jonás:	Yeah, for me it's a vice.
2nd interviewer:	If you don't play for a day, how do you feel?
Jonás:	I miss it, and I look for money wherever I can.

Lila recognizes that drugs lead many heterosexual men into homosexuality:

> Now, there's something else that society has never wanted to accept. Society doesn't realize that drugs make men sell themselves. No matter how macho they are, these men accept homosexual sex when they're drugged up . . . with a little alcohol and some drugs, they don't care if they go with a man or a woman.

Money and drugs have made the interviewees change the rules of *cacherismo*. Nóe agrees that drugs have made him "sell my ass" and live with a man. Augusto says the same thing, and admits that "When I need a hit really badly, I'll do anything, including licking and letting a guy have sex with me." Arnoldo says he has not yet reached that point, but he knows that "Many of them sell their asses to buy drugs." Mono makes fun of one of his co-workers who went with a client who only likes to penetrate, and came out with "ten thousand colones that he couldn't have earned if it weren't by taking it up the ass."

Some establish relationships with gays in order to live better or buy drugs. Tomás says he went to live with a man who could give him the luxuries he wanted. "People have started to say I'm gay, and to say I've become a queen, but since they don't support me, I don't care." Rodrigo feels the same conflict: "I want to get out of poverty and have the things I want. If a guy comes along and he's willing to give me that, I'll go live with him."

The need for money and drugs changes the sexual geography and the temporary nature of *cacherismo*. Some of the young men begin working in gay saunas to earn more money, while others pick men up in parks and even in gay bars. Others establish long-term relationships with men, even getting divorced and abandoning their children. Hugo admits he has become "more feminine because of my need for drugs and to get more men." Mario realizes that he has become an "old whore, and I still practice prostitution."

FAMILY AND CHILDREN

In theory, *cacheros* leave their profession when they get married and start a family. However, early paternity often becomes a reason for *cacheros* to continue as prostitutes and to look for more contacts with the homosexual world. The need to appear macho, and therefore the need to reproduce, ironically pushes these adolescents further into the gay lifestyle. Although most of them are under twenty, they already have children to feed. Marco is seventeen and has a four-month-old daughter. The money he used to spend on gambling and alcohol must now go to support his child.

2nd interviewer: What did you do with the 3,500 colones that you earned with a guy?

Marco:	That day I didn't have anything in the house for my girlfriend to . . .
2nd interviewer:	What does that mean—you didn't have anything?
Marco:	There was no food. I bought some milk that cost 1,200 [colones] for the baby, who I was most worried about.
2nd interviewer:	How old is the baby?
Marco:	At that time she was around two months old.
2nd interviewer:	Is canned milk expensive?
Marco:	Yeah, it's quite expensive because it's for newborns and this baby is very delicate and she can't drink just any milk . . . and that's what worries me when I don't have money.
2nd interviewer:	So, you look for clients because you don't have money for the baby?
Marco:	And for my girlfriend, too, because she didn't have anything to eat either.
2nd interviewer:	How long had it been since she had eaten?
Marco:	She'd had breakfast, but after that there was nothing in the house 'til I got home, if I'd made some money . . . or maybe not.

Marco is unable to save money, or even spend any on himself. "Jesus Christ! Life is so expensive. I earn just enough to feed my girlfriend and my child." The good thing about the child is that Marco has stopped using drugs in order to be able to feed her. "But now I have to go to saunas or parks to earn more money," he says.

Others, like René, find men to support them so that they can feed their families: "I have three children. I couldn't rely on prostitution because it's not stable. I found a regular homosexual lover who pays me at least a weekly salary so I can relax." This more permanent relationship means that he must accompany his lover to gay parties and even to "queer bars." René feels that people have started to look at him more as a "queer" than a *cachero*.

The responsibility of feeding a family has forced some to change their sexual practices. René recognizes that he has to kiss his male lover and perform oral sex on him, because "It's one thing to go to bed with a client and another to do it in a relationship. The guy expects affection and one has to give it to him. I'm not thrilled about it, but it's not about me anymore, and it's easier to do it if I know it's to feed my family." Pedro admits that he has let himself be penetrated since he had children: "I never sold my ass until I had to start buying so many things for the house. The pressure makes you agree to anything." Gerardo realizes that his money "is just not enough. With what I earned today, I bought rice, beans, lard, coffee, sugar, Gerber [baby food] . . . " To be able to buy cigarettes or beer, "I give blow jobs sometimes."

It is not only social relations and practices that vary, but also the temporary nature of the work. Some *cacheros* work in prostitution longer than they had planned. Family demands, which increase with the years, bind them to homosexuality. Mono has not been able to give up sex with men, even though he is considered "a veteran." Luis has become accustomed to his income from prostitution as an extra salary. The need to send his children to school "prevents me from giving up this lifestyle."

NEW DEMANDS

These young men are well aware of the reality of AIDS. When asked about the means of infection and transmission, all mentioned anal sex without a condom as the most dangerous practice. They also showed a high degree of awareness by noting the lack of consensus about the risks involved in oral sex and passive, versus active, anal sex. In theory, they always use condoms. This awareness of the disease is shared by clients, who have changed "their tastes," as Noé says. This change in tastes means that anal sex is not in such great demand and most clients just want "to be fondled," according to Arnoldo.

One of the effects of AIDS, then, has been the homogenization of sexual practices between *cacheros* and their clients. It is no longer possible to say with certainty who is active and who is passive in cases of mutual masturbation. According to Noé, "Before, the *cachero* was the one who penetrated the faggot, but now . . . I don't know . . . I couldn't tell you if he's the one who jerks off the faggot because it's not the same . . ." With practices becoming more similar, *cacheros* feel that their active role is disappearing: "I like to penetrate, but I hardly ever do it because I'm afraid of infecting my girlfriend," says Marco. "The truth is that you don't know anymore who's active and who's passive," he concludes.

Although client demand for passive anal sex in the brothel has declined, more clients want active sex (in the belief that it is safer), or try to get the prostitutes out of the brothel "so you're only with them," says Vernol. Thus, clients are willing to offer more money in order to "be sure that you're faithful to them," he says. They demand AIDS tests or that you move in with them to "be sure," says Tomás. There are now more opportunities to find an older man who will pay for your studies, support you, or offer you friendship and a place to live. José tells us about his friend, Esteban, who met an American. "He took him to Miami and now he's rolling in money and living the good life." Augusto is supported by a homosexual who has him "living like a king," in return for only having sex with him. "My partner doesn't care if I go to bed with my girlfriend, he just doesn't want me sleeping with other men."

This new demand for more long-term relationships is having an enormous impact on *cacheros'* lives. Some, like Alberto, try to fool others by claiming that "I live with my uncle." Others maintain their relationships with women to hide the fact that they have male lovers. However, their relationships with men remove them from their own communities, allow them to be seen by others, get them more involved in the gay community, and turn them into "homosexuals," the feared stigma of *cacherismo.*

ROMANTIC LOVE

The main dividing line between homosexuality and *cacherismo* is romantic love. *Cacheros* do not love their clients, nor do they establish emotional relationships with them. Sex relations must be seen—by clients and friends—as business transactions, in which one person sells and another buys. However, there is evidence that the romantic discourse of the lower classes is more tolerant then the middle classes of love between men.

To understand the impact of romantic love on *cacherismo,* it is necessary to analyze how this is expressed among the country's popular sectors. In the West, romantic love is seen as a drug and its means of expression varies among different cultures.[1] Among popular and marginal sectors of Costa Rican society, love is expressed by the things one is willing to do for the other person. The idea that two people in love possess "psychological depth" or "profound communication" comes more from the middle than the lower classes.[2] The belief that men and women are beings with complementary psychologies is also more predominant among the middle class. As far as poor people are concerned, men and women play different roles at home and at work, but do not inhabit different psychological worlds. Both must try to survive in a world of poverty through the power of their bodies, not their minds. Their way of expressing love is by taking care of each other. Passion is important but not crucial.

The fact that love is seen as a drug allows many barriers, including gender, to be broken. Jorge considers love to be "the most wonderful thing on earth," a kind of "madness in which you lose control and don't care who you get involved with." When asked how you know you are in love with another person, he answered that he feels "passion," "obsession," and that he "can't stop thinking about the person or doing things for the person." Alberto agrees that love wipes out all "loneliness" and "forgives" all wrongs. Arnoldo believes that when you are in love, you do "things you would never do otherwise." Tomás shared his thoughts that gender is irrelevant in the face of love: "Yes, you can fall in love with a man just like you would with a woman." Mono thinks that love "overcomes every obstacle," and forgives "every flaw." When you're in love," he says, "you forgive anything and you can even fall in love with a *pagador.*"

When asked about how they express love, the response was unanimous: by the things you do for the other person. Arnoldo buys his girlfriend chocolates. Noé caresses his wife. José cleans the house to show his lover that he cares. Augusto goes to the supermarket "once in a while." Pedro brings his wife a cup of coffee. Vernol does it with sex: "I show her that I love her with a good romp in the sack."

Pedro sums up their views of love and the way they show it:

1st interviewer:	Could you define love for me?
Pedro:	Love is everything, and I think that nobody can live in this world without love. Sex, love, and passion are all very different.
1st interviewer:	Tell me about that. Sex, love, and passion.
Pedro:	Love is something that's born in your spirit when you are deeply in love, and it doesn't matter if the woman is pretty or ugly. Sex is about pleasure, and passion can be about pleasure, too.
1st interviewer:	Do you think you have to work at love?
Pedro:	Yes, I think it's like a garden that you have to water every day. You have to show love, you can't just say "I love you."
1st interviewer:	And how do you show it?
Pedro:	With affection, caresses, little things . . .
1st interviewer:	Would it be the same for you to fall in love with a man as with a woman?
Pedro:	If I were in love, yes.

When the passion ends, a new kind of relationship develops which, although not as intense as at the beginning, still involves mutual care, company, and a life project.[3] Since *cacheros* usually conceive of love as the care two people give each other, rather than as the communication of intimate thoughts or the sharing of traumas (Hollywood-style), it is not difficult for them to fall in love with a man for whom they feel no passion.

Tomás recognizes this when he explains that the *pagador* who supports him treats him "so well and with such affection," that he is "delighted" with this relationship. Rodrigo said he felt he "would die" when the client who took care of him left him for someone else. Noé has lived with his *pagador* for seven years and when he was asked if he loved him, his answer was "yes." Jeffrey confesses that he could fall in love with a man "who was willing to keep me in nice clothes and other things."

Because they belong to a social class that does not associate love with the expression of intimate thoughts or the notion of complementary psychologies, *cacheros* are more liable to fall in love with a *pagador* who helps them survive and "bear life's burdens," as Marco says, regardless of whether that person is a man or a woman. When a *pagador* appears and establishes a relationship with a *cachero*, allowing him to transcend the stigma of prostitution, *cacherismo* is faced with its worst threat and the dividing line between commercial sex and homosexuality vanishes completely.

EMPATHY

One of the most important figures in the culture of this brothel is its owner, an effeminate gay man about fifty years old, who has been to prison for pimping. Lila lives from prostitution. He charges room fees of between 1,000 and 2,000 colones for every sexual encounter that takes place on his premises. For years, his business has consisted of recruiting young men from the street, pool halls, public parks, bathrooms, amusement parks, and other places. Some are brought here by friends or by clients who need a place to have sex.

The recruiting process is based solely on the young man's physical good looks. In other words, Lila does not look for any other sign that may convey an interest in prostitution. Some are invited to the brothel to be "tried out," as he says, to see how they measure up physically. Although clients prefer boys with big penises, this is not the only criterion for acceptance. Some boys are extremely handsome, and that is good enough. The owner obviously looks for young people in poor, but not destitute, areas of the capital. Since he is searching for pretty boys, he concentrates on areas whose populations have Spanish features rather than mestizo ones. Boys from very poor areas, where there are large migrant populations from Central America, are not sought after by his clients.

Lila recruits boys and youths ages ten to twenty years old. Tomás, for example, was brought here by a friend when he was just ten. The brothel owner taught him about oral sex, which is what he did until he was fourteen, when he moved on to penetration and other activities. Mono began working at the brothel at the age of fourteen and spent almost seven years there. Others start young, but live with their parents or other family members. There are even cases of mothers, such as Rodrigo's, who bring their sons to the brothel to prostitute themselves, and of brothers who recruit their siblings.

Young boys join the brothel without really knowing what is in store for them. Although their first sexual experience with a man makes quite an impression and scares them, none said they found it traumatic. One reason they find it relatively easy to accept homosexual practice is their heterosexual initiation.

When we asked them to recall their first sexual experiences, it turned out that all were initiated into sex by women much older than themselves. Mono, for example, was seduced by a cousin twenty years his senior. During a visit to the province of Limón, he was left alone with her in the house. She went to take a shower and called to him to rub soap over her. The ten-year-old boy did not understand what she was suggesting. He was scared when he saw her coming out of the shower naked and when she began to touch him. "I didn't even know what sex was, and the only thing I knew was how to jerk off. She started touching me and asked me to put more soap on her breasts. I got all heated up and since I didn't even know where to stick it, she grabbed it herself, and pushed it in."

The same thing happened to Noé, who was seduced by a friend of his mother's when he was only thirteen. "The woman invited me to have coffee with her, and after a while she took off her dress and asked me to lick her pussy." Hugo had his initiation with a girl of fifteen. He, however, was only eleven at the time. It was she who invited him to her house and "took off her clothes." For him, the experience was a total surprise, as "I didn't even know what a pussy was." Nevertheless, they had sex and continued to do so for several years. Carlos began his sex life with a prostitute very much his senior. His friends practically dragged him to her when he was twelve. The prostitute "had her legs open, and I'd never seen that 'thing' before . . . she told me to put it in there . . . that time I couldn't do anything, but I went back alone another time, and I did it."

If we compare these sexual experiences with the ones that Lila arranges, we find no major differences other than the gender of the initiators. By "modern" standards, these young men have been sexually abused both by men and women. By means of trickery and deceit, they were initiated at a very early age. However, during the interviews, none expressed hostility toward the men or women who abused them. While they do recognize the fear they felt, and even the shock of seeing sexual organs for the first time, they are not aware of any abuse. Violence is so endemic in their lives that it is difficult to imagine a relationship without it. When they tell their stories, they do it with a sense of mischief and remember the event as one of the best moments of their lives.

For this reason, no one harbors any resentment over his initiation into prostitution. Contrary to our expectations, we found no feelings of hostility toward Lila. Rather, there was a sense of gratitude for the protection they received when they had problems, the money that was lent to them, and the offer of a place to stay when they were thrown out of their homes. "Lila's like a mother to me," admits Mono. "I had no place to go, and he provided me with a home for seven years." Hugo feels the same way: "I never knew my father or my mother—I was raised by my grandparents. Lila has been both father and mother to me." Others who have never lived here are also fond of him: "That queen is the only person I can turn to in times of need." The young men know that Lila does not like them to take drugs and will not supply them. However, he tolerates them because "he can't do anything about it."

Lila, for his part, is not so certain of the young men's affections. When asked if he thinks they appreciate him, he answered, "Not really, because kids today are getting worse and worse—there's no more romance, or respect, or consideration." However, he does recognize that he does a lot for them:

> Well, a lot of people don't like me because they can't forgive me for liking money or being ambitious. I like nice things, but if I were rich, I'd be a humanist. I can't stand it when a man says he hasn't eaten all day or hasn't slept in days. I think about the times when I spent days on the street, starving to death, picking up a piece of dirty bread in Barrio Amón and having to eat it. Many of these kids have been thrown out onto the street and I can't refuse them a place to stay.

Lila is regarded as a father by many of them. Hugo explains it this way:

I see him as a father, because from the first moment I arrived here he treated me well. He gave me love, perhaps the love my father never gave me. He's given me what's missing in my life. When I have problems, I know where to turn. When my parents don't give me answers and maybe the solution has to do with my lifestyle, I can talk to Lila and he can help me. . . . I've often had problems with my girlfriend and I asked him what to do because I really didn't know, and he would tell me to do this or do that. . . . He is a kind of guide, that's the right word. Since I'm a whore, as people say, he tells me that when I'm with a client I should do this or that, be sensual in bed, and other things.

Unlike Hugo, Cerebrón says he does not love Lila, but he does appreciate him:

No, not love, but appreciation, yes. I appreciate Lila because he's a good person and other guys appreciate him, too. . . . He advises me to be careful about AIDS, not to be stupid. . . to use a condom, and to not let myself be intimidated by other men. . . . He likes to cuddle the guys, though I don't like him to touch me because he stinks and he doesn't bathe. But, in my toughest moments, he's given me a place to sleep and hasn't taken advantage of the situation to try and touch me. Sometimes we've slept in the same bed, and he's never tried anything.

Because Lila is a father-mother figure for those who have never had much support in their own homes, or those from poor homes without responsible fathers, they come to see homosexuality in a positive light. Unlike a study carried out in England, in which the prostitutes interviewed expressed hostility and disgust toward their clients, these young men do not discriminate against or feel resentment toward homosexuals.[4] Some, like Noé, consider them desirable, hard-working, creative people. Mono does not like queens, but he likes masculine gays and even considers them "his friends." Rodrigo says he cannot stand it when people make fun of gays: "I tell them that they shouldn't speak badly of anybody because you don't know what might happen to you as punishment."

The cordial atmosphere in Lila's brothel means homosexuals and *cacheros* have personal relationships that tend to blur the differences between them. Unlike many saunas, where the prostitutes barely speak to their clients, Lila's house is a familiar place where they tell jokes and share common problems. "I was amazed to hear what gays had to put up with for being effeminate as children. I never imagined there was so much pressure," admits Mono. In contrast to the rooms where sexual encounters take place, the brothel's living room or parlor provides a space for communication in the culture of *cacherismo.*

Cacheros hate homosexuality, but "love" homosexuals. This seems to be a contradiction in terms, but it is not. Ironically, the Catholic Church adopts the same position.

Chapter 5

Sodom and Gomorrah Revisited

One thing that is immediately apparent upon entering the brothel is its filth. The owner breeds dogs and, since he has no yard, the dogs defecate all over the house, in every room. Lila began breeding dogs six years ago, and now he has five of them. He claims that the dogs give him certain powers. "They're very large dogs—of a very intelligent breed. These dogs are mystical and it's all very strange. A person who died, who was murdered in 1971, had visions, and he told me that he saw six or eight dogs in this house and he warned me about dangers and things that could happen to me here."

Despite this canine magic, everyone notices the smell and the excrement. Lila admits that the house has no windows and there is nowhere for the stench to escape. Often, the first thing you see as you enter the house is excrement on the floor. Two of the dogs are always locked up inside a room next to the massage room.

The brothel workers are aware that the place is not very attractive and that they are losing clients as a result. However, they walk around the excrement as if it did not exist. One might assume that they are dirty, but that is not the case. On the contrary, they are well-dressed and attractive. Their indifference to the excrement that fills the place is a symptom of something more than slovenliness: the complete compartmentalization of their minds.

When one reads the interviews and compares what the interviewees say and what they actually do, it is easy to conclude that they are lying. There is evidence that practice differs greatly from the discourse of *cacherismo*. It is clear that condoms are seldom used at the brothel. We found no used condoms in the rooms or in the wastebaskets. Some interviewees insist that they use condoms, but most do not. Others admit that they do not like using them and neither do their clients.

The same is true of sexual practices. It is evident that the prostitutes practice both active and passive penetration. Very few admit to liking it, but those who are most aware say there are few who "don't take it." Thus, the assertion that *cacheros* are "active" is not true. The need for money, drugs, or even affection leads them to perform all kinds of practices and exposes them to infection.

Many sex workers have serious crack addiction problems. It is not true, as some of them claim, that their drug use is under control and that they do not steal or cheat to get drugs. When Lila's information is compared with the details provided by the prostitutes, it is apparent that many of them have had problems with the law and have been to prison.

Many of the stories told might well be considered lies. José tells us that he has only gone to bed with three men in his entire life. However, Lila says he does that in just one day. One day Mono claims he is twenty-three years old, another day he says he is twenty-five or twenty-seven. Noé says he has never been penetrated, but clients say he is "more wide open than the crater of Irazú [Volcano]." Hugo says that he has never had sex with a co-worker, while Ernesto tells us that clients request "performances" in which he performs oral sex on others.

However, instead of analyzing these stories as "lies," it would be better to treat them as "compartments" or mental drawers that the prostitutes create when there is no way to reconcile discourse contradictions and conflicting pressures. They have learned a discourse which should, in theory, protect them from being stigmatized as homosexuals. They know and accept the rules of the game. However, social pressures make it impossible to respect these norms. The dividing line between commercial sex and homosexuality is very thin. Thus, in order to continue seeing themselves as *cacheros*, they must find a way of separating the contradictions and the exceptions to the rule. The way to do that is simply to live with mental "drawers" or compartments that are separate and independent of each other.

These young men are well aware that when they pass through the brothel door, "We change into something else," as Arnoldo says.

This means that they have to be something very different on the street from what they are in the brothel. Here, they are men who have sex with men. On the street, they are lovers, boyfriends, and fathers. Jorge feels that "I have several personalities—there are a bunch of Jorges running around here." Miguel does not understand why "I'm one way in my house and another on the street." Carlos admits that "Nobody really knows me, not even my wife."

Variations in language use reflect the different aspects of their personalities. The way the interviewees speak inside the brothel differs from the way they speak outside. Rodrigo says he speaks "more femininely" in the brothel. This means he can share emotions—something he cannot do in the heterosexual pool hall. The guys like to mimic Lila and swing their hips like a queen. One of the jokes is to imitate a very effeminate man and talk like a queen. "On the street," Vernol tells us, "you walk like a man, speak more crudely, and you don't take any shit."

When they fall in love, enjoy sex with men, take drugs, or participate in orgies, their conduct deviates from their sexual discourse as *cacheros*. Pleasure dominates, and passion provokes "irrational" behavior, such as falling in love and not using condoms. In this way, distinct facets of the personality emerge that sometimes contradict each other.

CACHERISMO, CONDEMNATION, AND GUILT

We do not know where or when *cacherismo* originated. However, we do know that it has been condemned since biblical times and that it is associated with sin. One of the reasons *cacheros* feel unable to integrate this work into their lives is the long history of Christian hostility. The condemnation is so severe that it is impossible for them to counteract it. However, we introduced an allegory with the aim of studying the possibility of their questioning the Bible and seeing their profession in a different light.

In prebiblical times, homosexuality as we understand it today was unknown. Rather, what is associated with homosexual practice was in fact *cacherismo*: relations between men who did not cease to be men because they had sex with males. *Cacherismo* was tolerated in Greece and was not persecuted in itself. It was possible to be a free, respectable man, while being "active" with men and women. During this time, it was believed that one could only be either active or passive in sexual relations. The "passives" were looked down upon, but they did not constitute a separate sexual minority. They were, above all, slaves, young boys, eunuchs, prisoners of war, foreigners, and common prostitutes.

The distinction between who was active and who was passive was determined by class, not by sexual orientation. Free men with money could use other men as well as women, without experiencing discrimination for it. The passives had to consent, not because they were homosexuals, but because submission was linked to their social rank. One exception was the case of the cult prostitutes, who were treated with respect.

Hostility toward prostitution and homosexual practices came with Judeo-Christian ideas. The Old and New Testaments condemn them in four specific situations:[1]

1. When the right to asylum is violated (the story of Sodom and Gomorrah in which people wanted to abuse Lot's guests).
2. When it is associated with foreign practices (such as pagan religions in which homosexual acts were practiced in cult contexts).
3. When there was concern with low fertility and nonreproductive practices (such as wasting semen in masturbation).
4. When it is associated with pagan cults.

The interviewees do not know exactly which passages from the Bible are used against them, nor do they understand that homosexuality and prostitution in ancient times were very different from current practice. In fact, religious concerns arose for very specific reasons, which are not generally applicable to the *cacheros'* present activities. However, these young men are conscious of the condemnation and criticism leveled against them by priests and religious people, and their warnings that God will supposedly condemn them to hell. In this situation, it is impossible to have self-esteem, or to seek support for problems related to prostitution. It should come as no surprise, then, that prostitutes look to drugs or other addictions to relieve the guilt and pain of feeling condemned and discriminated against.

To analyze how they might see their work in a different light and free themselves from biblical fetters, we asked them to do the following visualization:

> People no longer feel pleasure in their genitals, but in their hair. They still have regular sexual relations for reproduction, but pleasure, true erotic pleasure, comes from having their hair washed, cut, and styled. Having your hair done is so pleasurable that some people enjoy it to excess and forget to eat or to have sexual relations. For this reason, the Bible has very prudently forbidden hair cuts. Delilah was condemned for cutting Samson's locks, which prevented him from having orgasms for several months. This passage is used to condemn hairstylists to Hell, as God disapproves of their methods. "He who cuts another's hair is an abomination," says one of the passages. Another even stronger one says, "There shall be no hairstylists in all of Israel. It is an insult to God." Another biblical passage tells the story of "Peluca and Gorra" (Wig and Cap), two towns in Canaan where people cut their hair so often that they went around with wigs and caps so as not to show the results. This bothered Yahweh so much that he struck them both down. In the New Testament, Paul was even stricter. In a letter to the sponsors of the Miss Universe pageant, he threatened, "None of the women who have their hair styled shall enter the kingdom of Heaven, neither shall the stylists, nor the braiders, nor the shampoo users, nor the users of conditioners, rollers, dyes, combs, brushes, and hair pieces."

Our aim was to show the prostitutes that their job might be seen just like any other if it were not for the long history of religious condemnation and negative attitudes toward sexuality. The fact that people condemn prostitution and homosexuality could be as morally significant as if they did it to a hairstylist. Why is it that massaging the scalp is regarded so differently from massaging genital organs? Why are people so worried about genitals while other organs can be massaged, stimulated, treated, touched, or caressed with no moral consequences? Why is it immoral to give someone an orgasm, while going to war, killing, and plundering are not condemned by religion?

The young men reacted very strongly to this exercise. Many of them said it was "blasphemous, irreverent, atheistic, and disrespectful." Luis, for example, says religion makes him feel so uncomfortable that he prefers "not to think about those things and condemn myself even further." Gerardo feels that it is wrong to "play" with the Bible and does not question that homosexuality has been condemned by the word of God. "He will forgive me when I leave this profession, but not if I show a lack of respect." Erick says the allegory "made me think, and what I thought scared me." Carlos thinks that doing this is like "messing with the devil." This is a natural reaction, since they already feel bad about their profession and do not wish to "offend God" in other ways, such as by reinterpreting the Bible. In other words, some of them feel so bad about what they do that they try to compensate by being overly religious.

However, others understood the message. Mono confesses that at the beginning the allegory bothered him, but afterward "I began to see that this really could be a business like any other, that it's a question of style or tradition." Jonás, who is not as religious, also got the message: "Of course, I don't know why people get so uptight about a hand job, and nobody says anything when politicians steal a whole bank like the Anglo [a reference to a state-run bank, the Banco Anglo, which went bankrupt amid political scandals]." Ernesto reacted this way: "Religion and morality is a load of crap. If you're poor, nobody helps you. I don't know why I should be ashamed of making a client feel good if it's nobody's business and I'm not stealing anything from anyone. How many politicians have gotten rich by robbing people? They do it, and the world kisses their ass. There was Calderón [Costa Rica's former President] staying at the house of a drug lord in Mexico, and nobody condemns him the way they do us. The worst we do is give pleasure to people that nobody loves." Lila puts it more eloquently: "This exercise seems like a good idea to me, because there's nobody more corrupt than the Church—they have the least right to open their mouths to condemn people who work. Why should that bunch of transvestites in black care if people enjoy sex? Why don't they sell that mansion in Rohrmoser [the luxurious residence of the Papal Nuncio] and give the money to the poor?"

Finally, one of them completely missed the point of the allegory: "Of course," says Carlos, "I always knew that God had condemned hairstylists 'cause they're all queens. They're sure to be condemned to Hell for being gossipy hens. That's why I go to a barber . . . never to one of those unisex queens."

AIDS PREVENTION

The interviewees were very knowledgeable about AIDS. All were aware of the main forms of transmission and prevention. During the first interviews, they claimed that they always used a condom when penetration was involved. However, they also had contradictory information on this point. Some, like Augusto, believe there is no risk of infection if they perform active penetration. Luis believes he is not at risk because he does not ejaculate inside his clients. Others believe that oral sex carries no risk of transmission. Although almost all the *cacheros* practice oral sex with their clients, none mentioned using a condom for this activity. There were other misconceptions, such as Cerebrón's idea that the real danger of infection is when you let yourself be penetrated by small penises. He believes that these "tear everything," whereas, "When it's a big dick, it goes in and stays in without tearing anything, and it doesn't make the sphincter bleed." Few use lubricants and they are not aware of the increased likelihood of the condom breaking if no lubricant is used. Some use saliva or petroleum jelly.

Cerebrón himself admitted that the condoms usually break. When we asked him why, he said it was because "My dick's very big and thick. It's not easy to find a condom that fits." However, when we asked him if he used a water-based lubricant to help put a condom on, his response was negative. The interviewees were even less knowledgeable about different brands of condoms and the fact that some are not suitable for anal sex and break easily. They tend to use condoms brought by the clients or provided by the owner, without knowing the differences in quality. They also have false notions about the protection afforded by washing the genitals with soap or applying alcohol after sexual intercourse. Although these precautions do not do any harm (with the exception of using Sanipine disinfectant as a lubricant to counteract foul odors), neither do they offer any protection against the AIDS virus.

Some of the *cacheros* know people who have contracted the AIDS virus and died. Despite this, they still do not always use condoms. Many of the interviewees claimed that they do use condoms, but that others do not. Copo, for example, has papilloma and has sought help from one of his clients who is a doctor. However, in the interview, he insisted that he does not have sex without a condom. Until our arrival, condoms were not available to prostitutes at Lila's house. According to Lila, he simply rents rooms and it is up to the clients to supply condoms. However, since we began supplying condoms, *cacheros* have started asking for them.

For Lila, AIDS is a distant threat. "There are worse problems facing all of us every day. My biggest fear is that the police will show up and I'll end up in jail again." When asked why he had not provided condoms previously, he admitted that "Many clients don't like them and I can't do anything about that. I rent rooms, and that's it." Miguel does not worry either: "My problem is eating. If a client offers me ten 'reds' [10,000 colones] for sex, and he doesn't want me to use a condom, it's up to him." Others claim they always use condoms or that they only practice masturbation. However, their co-workers contradict their affirmations and tell us that they, too, make exceptions.

Married *cacheros*, or those who live with women, are usually more careful, since they are fearful of transmitting venereal diseases, especially AIDS, to their women. Given that they dislike using condoms with their wives or girlfriends, the price of not using them with their clients is greater. Nevertheless, many of those who have female partners who know about their work do not always use condoms. Mono claims that he will not do anything without a condom, but his co-workers say he has sex with married men who do not like using condoms.

Since we could not conduct this study and simply observe the situation without doing something to help, we told Lila from the beginning that we would supply these young men with condoms. He agreed to give one to each worker who requested one. As a result, condoms have begun to circulate more often around the house. The evidence can be seen in the wastebaskets and in the fact that the young men come to ask for them when a client requests penetration. According to Ernesto, now that condoms are available, he has begun to use them often. Mono and Hugo say they request them directly from Lila. "If I'm going to give it to a client, I ask for a condom," admits Cerebrón. But despite some initial success, not all *cacheros* are so assertive. Mono says that he sometimes has to "stop" a client who asks him not to use a condom. "I can afford to tell him to go to hell, if I have to. However," he adds, "many guys here can hardly talk, much less stand up to a client."

Other factors, such as crack and alcohol consumption, also influence condom use in the brothel. *Cacheros* generally lose the ability to negotiate when they are drunk or high. Mono confesses, "I don't remember any of what I did yesterday. I smoked three joints with this guy and I know I spent the whole night with him. But if you ask me what I did, I swear I don't remember a thing." Marco recognizes that when he was "on drugs, I never turned down money and I wasn't difficult with anybody."

Another factor has to do with the difference between romantic love and sexual work. *Cacheros* differentiate between what they do for love and what they do for money. For love, "You trust and sacrifice for the other person," says Daniel. For money, "You can say what you want," says Erick. In other words, *cacheros* use protection with their clients but not with their lovers, whether they are men or women. "When I'm in love like I am now," says Jonás, "I show my woman that I love her and trust her. We'll never use a condom." Ernesto does the same with men: "That regular client I told you about had a four-year relationship with me, and I never used a condom with him. If he was giving me money and supporting me . . . how could I show distrust? According to him, I was faithful." Love, according to the interviewees, is shown by trust, faithfulness, and by not using protection.

Interviewer:	When you're in love, what do you think about using condoms?
Marco:	I don't think about them. I don't like to use condoms when I'm in love.
Interviewer:	You don't use them?

Marco:	No, I don't. I like the sensation of feeling the woman I love without a rubber separating us.
Interviewer:	Is it a barrier?
Marco:	For me, it's a barrier when I'm in love with a woman. For pleasure, yeah, I use a condom, but for love, no, I risk everything.
Interviewer:	What do you mean by "risk everything"?
Marco:	Everything, like AIDS, whatever . . .
Interviewer:	Do you think that being in love can protect you from AIDS?
Marco:	No, it can't protect me, but I feel happy when I do it without a condom.
Interviewer:	Would it be the same with a man?
Marco:	Exactly the same, no different.
Interviewer:	Have you ever fallen in love with a man?
Marco:	No, I haven't. This first time it's been a woman. I don't know if in the future it will be a man. Fate is so weird that you never know.
Interviewer:	But it would be the same?
Marco:	Yes.

The interviewees make exceptions for known or regular clients. Part of being intimate is doing it without a condom:

> I used a condom at the beginning with this client. But after the fourth time, he asked me to do it without a condom. I told him I didn't want to, that it was dangerous. But he said he really liked me and he wanted to continue just with me. He started to give me really good head, and when I realized what was happening, he'd already gone ahead and put it in without a condom. After a while, I asked him if he wanted to keep going or stop. He told me it felt so good, so full, that I should keep going.

Not only does the definition of intimacy affect condom use, but also the *cacheros'* desire to have children. As we have seen, most are fathers and had children when they were very young. Many want to have more children, either because they like the idea, or to demonstrate their manhood. Gerardo has four and he still wants more: "I like being a dad. I don't use condoms because I want more children."

Another factor has to do with the lack of solidarity among *cacheros*. They are a minority with few channels of communication among themselves, since they tend to regard each other as competition. Cerebrón complains that many of them charge "any ridiculous price," which brings down the prices of the rest. "I yelled at Emilio about letting himself be penetrated for 2,000 colones. 'Don't be a fool!' I told him. 'Don't you see that clients are taking advantage of us?'" The same thing happens with condom use. "Look," says Hugo, "I always try to use a condom. . . . but what can we do when this seventeen-year-old punk shows up and, for five hundred colones more, doesn't use one?" Mono feels the same way: "The youngest guys are the most sought-after, the most unaware, and the most desperate for money. They're the ones who will do anything without a condom."

Compartmentalization is another reason why condoms are seldom used. *Cacheros* live in different worlds with little connection between them. In Costa Rica, there are two parallel AIDS-prevention campaigns. The official campaign, directed at the heterosexual population, emphasizes fidelity and monogamy as means of prevention. The unofficial version, developed by ILPES, places emphasis on condom use and is aimed more at the gay community. There is no specific campaign for bisexual sex workers, and neither of the two existing initiatives has attempted to regulate pornography to integrate a message of "safe sex." Pornography, which remains illegal in this country, has not adapted to the reality of AIDS, or, if it has, it is not what these young men are looking at. Many of the available movies probably came out decades ago, before AIDS, and do not include condom use.

Instead of assimilating the message to always use condoms, both with men and women, *cacheros* combine the two campaigns. In theory, they accept the use of condoms in their homosexual relations, but not in their heterosexual ones. Therefore, the notion of prevention becomes compartmentalized in the same way as their sex lives. Mario, for example, says he uses a condom with men, but "I'm faithful to my woman because I think that's the best way to protect us both." Carlos agrees: "I'm faithful to my girlfriend. Condoms are for clients."

THE END OF THE HOUSE

For many years, Lila dreamed about a promise made by a Dominican client to lend him the money to buy a better house. It was never clear why the client wanted to help Lila. Nor do we know the nature of the relationship between these two characters. "He appreciated me and wanted to do me a favor. He had a good time with the guys I introduced him to," Lila explained. A client told us that this friend "felt sorry" for the brothel owner, and thought he deserved something better and that if he had a nice, clean house, he would be able to escape from poverty. Some speculate that the Dominican was a street kid. "He's a good-looking guy. He must have been as pretty as a picture when he was young," says another client. Out of friendship, the client was willing to make Lila's dream come true: "to get me out of this roach motel and into a nice place." He promised to give Lila the money after a trip abroad.

Lila had already chosen a house, located just four blocks from the present one, and costing ten million colones. The Dominican promised a low interest rate, with a reasonable payment plan. However, fulfillment of this promise was a long time coming. La Preciada had already warned Lila that he was living in a fantasy world: "You're crazy if you think he's going to lend you that money. Why don't you come down off that cloud and think about how you're going to clean the house?" Lila, for his part, believed that La Preciada was jealous of him. "That queen just wants to see me humiliated in this pigsty. She turns green with envy just thinking about how I might have a better house and how I wouldn't need to depend on her, so she couldn't insult me."

But the money never materialized. Months passed and finally Lila decided to face the truth and call Santo Domingo. This time his friend set him straight: "I don't have fifty thousand dollars to lend you. So, stop calling to bother me." Lila was in crisis for several days. The opportunity that he had hoped would save his life came tumbling down like a house of cards: "I'm completely depressed. I don't know what to do. I'll never have a decent house," he said bitterly. For several weeks, "Lila cried like a baby, prostrate before the statue of Changó," Mike explains.

It was the beginning of the end. Lila did not have the resources to become a refined madam. The money he earned renting rooms had slipped through his fingers just as fast as the *cacheros* spend theirs. According to La Preciada, "Feeding this bunch of punks has cost him a fortune. He never learned to be a madam first and a mother second. As a mother he's ended up poorer than Mother Theresa. . . . maybe poorer because she spends all that money on building convents."

Had Lila already decided to close the brothel before the Dominican betrayed him? From the time we began this investigation, Lila knew that once the book was published, the house would be in danger. No matter how much we tried to conceal the location of the house and change the names of the characters, some people would recognize them. Any person harboring a grudge could very easily call the police and give them the address. "With all the jealous people around, someone's going to denounce me, if I get famous," he warned us.

Deep down, Lila wanted to finish with the brothel. "I'm tired of this business. I'd like to have done something better with my life and not have to live with the terror of ending up in jail again. That's my worst nightmare." When the Dominican told Lila he could not lend him the money, Lila knew his life as a madam was at an end, and so was his house. "I want to grow old in a dignified manner, to repent and be forgiven, and then become a saint, like Eva Perón. After I'm dead, they'll say I was generous, that I fed the hungry, that my foundation clothed the needy, that Lila went straight to heaven and didn't need a visa to get in." In closing, he sings out of tune:

> Santa Lila, Santa Lila. Don't cry for me Costa Rica. I still love you; don't keep your distance. And as for fortune, and as for fame, I never invited them in, though it seemed to the world they were all I desired. They are illusions; they are not the solution they promise to be; the answer was here all the time.

During the writing of this book, Lila began to paint and fix up the house. One day he started to fix up the back room where the interviews took place. Then, he decided to try to put a stop to the flooding problems by building a roof over the patio that backs onto the kitchen. Another day, he decided to paint the house. His goal was to close the house as a center of prostitution and do something else. "I don't know . . . all your questions, when I sat down to think about my life, about living in danger, about going to jail, all this had to do with closing the brothel."

Our protagonist is an intelligent man, who, given the opportunity, might have done something better with his life. He is shrewd, introspective, analytical, and cultured. However, his life has been no bed of roses. His addiction to sex has combined with the young men's addiction to drugs and the clients' addiction to danger. He is no less trapped than they are, nor is he a simple exploiter of *cacheros* and their clients. Lila is simply one more victim of addiction. "I haven't made any money or gotten out of this dump. The guys have gotten as much money from me as I've gotten out of them," he concludes. Unbridled sexual desire became a substitute for many things he never had, and it was something he never could control.

Finally, it must be recognized that Lila has contributed to the realization of a dream: the creation of a refuge for young prostitutes. In June 1997, El Salón, the first club for sex workers in Costa Rica, was opened. It is a prevention project that offers *cacheros* condoms, AIDS prevention workshops, work alternatives, twelve-step programs, and social activities. We must remember that none of this would have been possible without Lila. No other center of prostitution would have been willing to cooperate in this kind of campaign or allowed us to come in and conduct interviews over such a long period of time. Although he does not admit it, perhaps Lila loves *cacheros* more than he imagines, and, at the end of his career, wanted to leave them something good. "I'll be a saint, the only madam who launched a plan to help prostitutes and protect them from other vipers like me. There are very few people who would kill the goose that lays the golden eggs."

Glossary

active and passive: Refers to anal penetration: the person who penetrates is active, and the one who is penetrated is passive.

cachero   Heterosexual man who has sexual relations with other men.

dyke: Lesbian.

give head: Perform oral sex on a man.

go down on: Perform oral sex.

landing: Sexual relations.

pagador: A patron, usually an older man who befriends and buys sex from young men.

sugar daddy: A man who financially supports a younger one in exchange for sex.

Notes

Introduction

1. K. J. Dover, *Greek Homosexuality* (Cambridge, MA: Harvard University Press, 1978).

2. Donald J. West, *Male Prostitution* (Binghamton, NY: Harrington Park Press, 1994).

3. Vern L. Bullough, *Sexual Variance in Society and History* (Buffalo, NY: Prometheus Books, 1993); Vern L. and Bonnie Bullough, *Women and Prostitution* (Buffalo, NY: Chicago Phoenix Edition, 1992).

4. J. Carrier, "Mexican Male Bisexuality" in F. Klein and Timothy Wolf (eds.), *Two Lives to Lead: Bisexuality in Men and Women* (Binghamton, NY: Harrington Park Press, 1993).

5. Ellyn Kaschak and Sara Sharrat, "Los roles sexuales comparados: Sorpresas en Costa Rica." *Rumbo Centroamericano* (July 11–17, 1995), pp. 15-17.

6. D. Halpern, *A Hundred Years of Homosexuality* (London: Routledge, 1990).

7. R. J. McMullen, *Enchanted Boy* (London: Gay Men's Press, 1989).

8. West, *Male Prostitution,* p. xii.

9. S. E. Caukins and M. A. Coombs, "The psychodynamics of male prostitution," *American Journal of Psychotherapy* (30, 1976), pp. 441-451.

10. D. Allen, "Young male prostitutes: A psychological study," *Archives of Sexual Behavior* (9, 399–426, 1980).

11. T. Robinson, "London's homosexual male prostitutes: Power, peer group and HIV," Project Sigma (Working Paper 12, Polytechnic of the South Bank, London, 1989).

12. West, *Male Prostitution,* p. 324.

13. Jacobo Schifter, *La Formación de una Contracultura. Homosexualismo y SIDA en Costa Rica* (San José, Costa Rica: Editorial Cuaycán, 1979, p. 109).

14. Ibid., p. 109.

15. W. Churchill, *Homosexual Behavior Among Males: A Cross Cultural and Crosss–Species Investigation* (New York: Hawthorn Books, 1967).

16. A. C. Kinsey, W. B. Martin, and P. E. Gebhard, *Sexual Behavior in the Human Male* (Philadelphia: W. B. Saunders, 1948).

17. B. W. Blumstein and P. Shwartz, "Bisexual Women" in J. Wiseman (ed.), *The Social Psychology of Sex* (New York: Harper and Row, 1976), pp. 145–162.

18. C. A. V. Warren, *Identity and Community in the Gay World* (New York: John Wiley and Sons, 1974).

19. J. Bode, *View from Another Close: Exploring Bisexuality in Women* (New York: Hawthorn Books, 1976).

20. F. Klein, *The Bisexual Option* (New York: Arbor House, 1978).

21. C. McInnes, *Loving Them Both: A Study in Bisexuality and Bisexuals* (London: Dawson, 1973).

22. J. C. Scott, *Wives Who Love Women* (New York: Walker, 1978).

23. F. Klein, "Are you sure you are heterosexual? Or even bisexual?" *Forum Magazine* (pp. 41-45, 1980).

24. *Cachero* is a word for which there is no English translation, with the closest word being "top man." However, *cacheros* are not considered homosexual or bisexual; they are seen as heterosexual men who have sex with other men for money or because of a lack of women.

Chapter 1

1. Costa Rican newscaster.

2. Latin American talk-show.

3. Jacobo Schifter and Johnny Madrigal, *Hombres que Aman Hombres* (San José, Costa Rica: Editorial Ilep-Sida, 1992).

4. Jacobo Schifter and Johnny Madrigal, *Las Gavetas Sexuales del Costarricense* (San José, Costa Rica: Editorial IMEDIEX, 1996).

5. Donald J. West, *Male Prostitution* (Binghamton, NY: Harrington Park Press, 1993).

Chapter 2

1. Michel Foucault, *Historia de la Sexualidad 1—La Voluntad de Saber* (México: Siglo XXI, 1977).

2. Jacobo Schifter and Johnny Madrigal, *Las Gavetas Sexuales del Costarricense* (San José, Costa Rica: Editorial IMEDIEX, 1996).

3. An example of the distinct meanings given to common words is that of "sodomy." For the youths, sodomy is not anal penetration, but masturbation. "Gay" is not a homosexual man who has come out of the closet and affirms his identity, but rather a transvestite.

4. Schifter and Madrigal, *Las Gavetas Sexuales del Costarricense.*

Chapter 4

1. M. Scott Peck, *The Road Less Traveled* (New York: Touchstone, 1978).

2. Jacobo Schifter and Johnny Madrigal, *Las Gavetas Sexuales del Costarricense* (San José, Costa Rica: IMEDIEX, 1996).

3. Robert A. Johnson, *We: Understanding the Psychology of Romantic Love* (San Francisco: Harper and Row Publications, 1983).

4. Donald J. West, *Male Prostitution* (Binghamton, New York: Harrington Park Press, 1993).

Chapter 5

1. Jacobo Schifter, *Hombres Que Aman Hombres* (San José, Costa Rica: Editorial ILEP-SIDA, 1992).

Index

Page numbers followed by the letter "f" indicate figures.

Order Your Own Copy of
This Important Book for Your Personal Library!

LILA'S HOUSE
Male Prostitution in Latin America

_____ in hardbound at $29.95 (ISBN: 0-7890-0593-X)

_____ in softbound at $12.95 (ISBN: 1-56023-943-3)

COST OF BOOKS_____	☐ **BILL ME LATER:** ($5 service charge will be added)
	(Bill-me option is good on US/Canada/Mexico orders only;
OUTSIDE USA/CANADA/	not good to jobbers, wholesalers, or subscription agencies.)
MEXICO: ADD 20%_____	
	☐ Check here if billing address is different from
POSTAGE & HANDLING_____	shipping address and attach purchase order and
(US: $3.00 for first book & $1.25	billing address information.
for each additional book)	
Outside US: $4.75 for first book	
& $1.75 for each additional book)	Signature_____
SUBTOTAL_____	☐ **PAYMENT ENCLOSED: $**_____
IN CANADA: ADD 7% GST_____	☐ **PLEASE CHARGE TO MY CREDIT CARD.**
STATE TAX_____	☐ Visa ☐ MasterCard ☐ AmEx ☐ Discover
(NY, OH & MN residents, please	☐ Diners Club
add appropriate local sales tax)	Account # _____
FINAL TOTAL_____	Exp. Date _____
(If paying in Canadian funds,	
convert using the current	Signature _____
exchange rate. UNESCO	
coupons welcome.)	

Prices in US dollars and subject to change without notice.

NAME _____

INSTITUTION _____

ADDRESS _____

CITY _____

STATE/ZIP _____

COUNTRY _____ COUNTY (NY residents only) _____

TEL _____ FAX _____

E-MAIL_____
May we use your e-mail address for confirmations and other types of information? ☐ Yes   ☐ No

Order From Your Local Bookstore or Directly From
The Haworth Press, Inc.
10 Alice Street, Binghamton, New York 13904-1580 • USA
TELEPHONE: 1-800-HAWORTH (1-800-429-6784) / Outside US/Canada: (607) 722-5857
FAX: 1-800-895-0582 / Outside US/Canada: (607) 772-6362
E-mail: getinfo@haworthpressinc.com
PLEASE PHOTOCOPY THIS FORM FOR YOUR PERSONAL USE.

BOF96